Non-I

Yuri Lotman

Translated and annotated by Caroline Lemak Brickman

Edited by Evgenii Bershtein

Afterword by Caroline Lemak Brickman
and Evgenii Bershtein

DALKEY ARCHIVE PRESS
Champaign / London / Dublin

Originally published in Russian as *Ne-memuary* in the book *Lotmanovskii sbornik* by Garant, Moscow, 1995

Copyright © The Estonian Semiotics Repository Foundation

Translation copyright © 2013 Caroline Brickman and Evgenii Bershtein

First edition, 2014

All rights reserved

Library of Congress Cataloging-in-Publication Data

Yuri Lotman, IU. M. (IUrii Mikhailovich), 1922-1993.
    [Ne-memuary. English]
    Non-memoirs / Yuri Lotman ; translated and annotated by Caroline Lemak Brickman; edited by Evgenii Bershtein; afterword by Caroline Lemak Brickman and Evgenii Bershtein. -- First edition.

    pages cm
    Includes bibliographical references.
    ISBN 978-1-56478-996-9 (pbk. : acid-free paper)
    1. Lotman, IU. M. (IUrii Mikhailovich), 1922-1993. 2. Critics--Russia--Biography. 3. Semioticians--Russia--Biography. 4. Culture--Semiotic models. 5. Semiotics and literature. I. Brickman, Caroline Lemak, translator. II. Bershtein, Evgenii, editor. III. Title.
    P85.L68A3 2014
    410.92--dc23
    B

                     2014016369

Partially funded by a grant by the Illinois Arts Council, a state agency

www.dalkeyarchive.com

Cover: design and composition by Mikhail Iliatov
Printed on permanent/durable acid-free paper

TABLE OF CONTENTS

I.

ONE AFTERNOON IN December 1992, in Tartu, Estonia, Yuri Mikhailovich Lotman reluctantly sat down to dictate his memoirs to Jelena Pogosjan, his assistant, over a pot of tea. Before his wife, Zara Grigorievna Mints, died in 1990, he had promised her that he would write the story of his life, and it was in memory of her that he embarked on this project. This December afternoon was the first of twelve dictation sessions during which the initial draft of *Non-Memoirs* was created between Lotman and Pogosjan. The sessions were spread out over that winter and into the spring of 1993—the last spring of Lotman's life. He could no longer write himself, due to a series of debilitating strokes and the weakness brought on by kidney cancer, and so had grown accustomed to the process of dictation and transcription to produce *Non-Memoirs* as well as his final theoretical works.

Pogosjan took notes by hand while Lotman spoke, and later typed up her notes and read them back to him, writing down his spoken corrections in the margins. When he died in October 1993, Pogosjan added a couple of annotations to the manuscript and sent it to Lotman's son, Mikhail Lotman, for final editing and publishing. The younger Lotman, in consultation with Pogosjan, arranged the sections of the manuscript chronologically and, together with his father's sister, Lidiya Lotman, added further editorial annotations before publication.

The first edition of the text was published as *Ne-memuary*, or *Non-Memoirs*, in 1995, in a collection of works by and about Lotman called *Lotmanovskii sbornik*. A second edition was published in 1999 by the prominent literary scholar Boris Egorov as an appendix to his biography of Lotman, *The Life and Works of Yuri M. Lotman* (*Zhizn' i tvorchestvo Yu. M. Lotmana*). The third edition, which has been used for this translation, was published in 2003 in a collection called *Vospitanie dushi*, as part of a complete series of Lotman's works put out by the Iskusstvo – St. Petersburg Publishing House. The memoirs have also been published online. Although *Non-Memoirs* has come out in Italian and (partially) in Spanish, this is the first English translation.

In its published form, *Non-Memoirs* is divided into seven sections of varying length. The five shorter sections concern themselves with a single anecdote or theme (body lice on the front, an encounter with a hare, a "totally Bulgakovian" episode, a visit from the KGB, Tartu School politics); the two longer sections provide the narrative backbone of the memoirs, tending to treat the passage of time, rather than a single event (school and front line life, the end of the war and postwar university life). We may assume that Lotman himself was responsible as a storyteller for the artistry of the shorter episodes; however, the longer sections and the arc of the text as a whole take their narrative shape posthumously: the text's editors collated the initial manuscript in accordance with their memory of Lotman's biography.

II.

BORN ON FEBRUARY 28, 1922, in Petrograd (now St. Petersburg), Lotman came of age in a family of Jewish intellectuals during an era characterized by Stalin's purges and repressions. He was drafted into the Red Army—then the national army of the Soviet Union—in 1940 and served through 1945 in combat. He came back as a decorated soldier to finish his studies in philology at Leningrad State University, but a Jewish scholar couldn't find work in the midst of Stalin's postwar anti-Semitic campaign against "cosmopolitanism." Finally he found a position at a pedagogical institute affiliated with Tartu University in Estonia—a university remote enough (and in a new enough province, as Estonia had only been annexed in 1940) from the Soviet center that its administration did not consider his Jewishness a liability. In 1950, Lotman moved to Tartu and married his university sweetheart Zara Grigorievna Mints (1927-1990). Together, they had three sons.

While working at the teaching institute, Lotman also began to teach classes at Tartu University. By 1954 he was a full-time faculty member. Once again, Tartu's distance from the Soviet political centers proved to be a stroke of luck: in large part thanks to the university's situation on the margins of the USSR, for the next four decades—and even after his death—Lotman and his colleagues were able to build an institution of cultural, historical, philological, and linguistic scholarship that would gain world renown.

Lotman began his career as a historian of eighteenth- and nineteenth-century culture and literature. Once established at Tartu, he began to correspond with structuralist scholars in Moscow, and he started lecturing and publishing on semiotics in the 1960s. His work came under political scrutiny and academic attack, and at first only his own university would publish him. The 1970s brought a number of works that combined Lotman's semiotic writings with his earlier interest in culture, and in the 1980s he developed a theory of culture and language based in semiotics. In 1980 Lotman also published his well-known commentary to Aleksandr Pushkin's novel in verse, *Eugene Onegin,* and a year later his equally famous biography of Pushkin.

By the 1980s Lotman had gained international fame as a semi-otician and cultural historian. He became a television personality in 1988, with a series of popular televised lectures on the culture of Russian nobility. Since then, his authority as a scholar has only grown, extending beyond his work and theories to the very image of his face, down to his distinctive ears, nose, and mustache.

III.

MANY OF LOTMAN'S scholarly interests are evident in his memoirs: motifs of history and historiography, language, culture, and above all semiotics are the threads holding these stories together. However, in addition to witnessing the scholar employ his theoretical tools in his reminiscences of war and youth, we can also see how Lotman's wartime experience impacted the patterns of his later theoretical thought. Wartime metaphors abound in his work on semiotics, culture, and systems of communication. Lotman's portraits of the front lines often bring life and detail to theoretical concepts such as the semiosphere (a posited semiotic space within which all languages function) and the explosion (an interaction between two or more linguistic systems that ruptures the semiotic space between them, simultaneously destroying and generating meaning).

Much of Lotman's theoretical work, especially his later work, asserts that literature, culture, and history are fundamentally *collective* endeavors. His memoirs are primarily war stories: they have been told and re-remembered many times; they rely on the relationship between teller and listener to take and change their form. Lotman did not consider the text of *Non-Memoirs* a complete work unto itself. Nor is it an authoritative statement of history. Instead, it invites its readers—as it has already invited its transcribers, commentators, editors, and translators—to step in as co-authors and help create in it a collective historiography.

Caroline Lemak Brickman
Evgenii Bershtein

NON-MEMOIRS

I.

IN 1939 VOROSHILOV announced in one of his speeches—I no longer remember which one—that the military deferment granted to students was unjust, and so all students were denied it. I was in my first year studying in the Philology Department, a subdivision of Russian Language and Literature.

Entering university had entirely changed my life. I'd had a hard time in grade school, especially in the sixth and seventh grades. I had an ongoing conflict with the Russian Language and Literature teacher—I don't remember what her name was—and with some members of the class. One episode occurred when we were studying *The Government Inspector*. The teacher assigned roles to the class, and we read it aloud. I had to read Khlestakov. For the first time in my life I felt that I had an artistic inclination. And I remember how I cried out my lines with this special feeling: "They're bringing it!" The class clapped; the teacher said that I played Khlestakov very well indeed, because it was in my nature. I was terribly insulted. The next year, beginning with the ninth grade, we had a new teacher. Dmitrii Ivanovich Zhukov, a mathematician, became our class instructor, and Efim Grigorievich taught literature and Russian.

I suddenly realized that school could be interesting. In the ninth and tenth grades, to my surprise, I became a good student. Trigonometry enthralled me, math was suddenly no longer a torment, and literature unexpectedly became an especially ardent passion. Dostoevsky engrossed me. By this time I had already read all of Tolstoy (the edition with the black volumes—a supplement to the journal *Ogonyok*). I read *War and Peace* several times (I still read it continuously, and I don't know how many times I've read it through—I probably know it by heart). Tolstoy's tales especially affected me.

After class Efim Grigorievich and I would talk for long periods about Dostoevsky. At the same time another important event occured in my life: Lida started at university. Students began to come over to our house (Lida's group of friends would study for tests at our place). That year (although this year was the last) they still weren't accepting the children of civil servants (what they called children "from non-laboring families") at the university without previous industrial experience. There had to be a minimum of two years' training in industry. So, of the students in Lida's group, only she and her friend Nelly Rabkina had come straight from high school. Lida would usually study for tests with a little group of friends in our big apartment on Nevsky. In addition to Lida and Nelly there was a young man, Naumov (he later married Nelly, who, after marrying, taught and wrote articles under the name Naumova)—he was enterprising, and interested in Soviet literature, which at the time did not seem to be a scholarly subject, but rather something too new for academic study. Naumov carefully concealed that he was from a "repressed" family[1], and had already stepped onto the path of a Party career. Later, on that path, he managed to do well for himself as the head of a Leningrad publishing house. But for me the most decisive acquaintance was with another of Lida's friends: Anatoly Mikhailovich Kukulevich. After he fulfilled two or three years of the required labor practice training as an agronomist, he enrolled at Leningrad University and studied simultaneously in the Russian Department under the advisorship of Grigory Aleksandrovich Gukovsky and in Classics under Ivan Ivanovich Tolstoy. Gukovsky promised this brilliantly gifted and charming man an exceptional academic future after Kukulevich managed to publish several articles on Gnedich in the "Scholarly Proceedings" of Leningrad University and a chapter in the just-released collection *The History of Russian Literature*. He was killed at the Leningrad front in late 1941. He survived the retreat from the border to Leningrad, and once he ran over in his military uniform to drop in on my family, merry and wild—and only just broken out of military encirclement.

He had great influence on me. Until then I had planned to study entomology. In this endeavor I was supported by a friend of Kukulevich's, Sasha (Aleksandr Sergeevich) Danilevsky, a future professor and entomologist, the great-great-grandson of Pushkin, a descendant of Gogol's sister, and a direct relation of the writer Danilevsky. In profile he did rather remind one of the young Gogol and of the Pushkin depicted in N. N. Ge's painting *Pushkin at Mikhailovskoe* (Ge's

---

1 His brother, an aircraft designer, was arrested. (Lidiya Lotman's note)

Pushkin is strange: he doesn't much resemble Pushkin, but does look a bit like Sasha Danilevsky). It was not without Sasha Danilevsky's charm that I decided to become an entomologist and diligently read specialized literature. The mysterious world of insects, which I find intimidating and captivating, arouses a strange feeling in me even now—I think it is precisely insects, with their exceptionally slow evolution and startling power to survive, who will be the final population on our planet. There is no doubt that they are endowed with their own intellectual world, but that world will always be closed to us. And so I "migrated" from insects to Russian literature. Under the influence of Efim Grigorievich and Tolya Kukulevich, an interest in literature and, more broadly, general philology awoke in me. I began to study Greek (which I have now, unfortunately, entirely forgotten).

We were all growing up quickly. The parents of maybe ten of my classmates were arrested. The father of Bor'ka Lakhman, my best friend, was arrested and then shot. He was a prominent Party worker and the director of the Institute of Low Electric Currents. A portrait of Rykov hung in their house—a portrait given to them, according to Bor'ka, by Rykov himself. The execution of his father and the exile of his mother and sister (Bor'ka stayed in the apartment alone, untouched) did not affect our friendship. We continued to get together in the evening at his apartment, which by then was already empty, or over at our place, and we would both say eagerly that soon war would come. It sounds absurd now. Once it began in Spain, we felt the entire inevitability of the war. There is nothing more ridiculous to me than the talks of Hitler's sudden and "treacherous" attack. Perhaps only Stalin himself was intoxicated by what he considered a very cunning maneuver, and forced himself to believe that the alliance with Hitler had eliminated the threat of war, but none of us believed it. In truth, some girls (I'm jumping ahead by more than a year, I'm skipping the Spanish war, I'm remembering when Ribbentrop came to Moscow) suddenly began to wear their hair like Aryan maidens (in rollers), and one of Lida's classmates said, when she was over at our place, that Ribbentrop had "inescapably influencing eyes." But Germanophilia was so brief at least among that circle about which I can speak with personal experience[2] that it gripped only girls: high schoolers and coeds.[3]

And though I don't remember whether it was Bor'ka Lakhman or myself who said these words, I remember them as if it were now: "At that point, it'll never occur to anyone to consider who's a Trotskyite and who's a Bukharinist; everyone will be a soldier on the front."

---

2 In the future I won't repeat this kind of qualification about my own subjectivity, but it should always be kept in mind, even when I'm talking about newspaper reports and political events.

3 Later, there was a text, folkloric among partisans, which had been reworked from the song "Dark burial mounds are sleeping . . ." (popular in the last year before the war, from the movie *A Great Life*). Part of it went like this:

> You do your hair up
> In German kitty style (sometimes it was "girly style" or "birdie style"),
> You rouge your lips (it used to be such depravity!),
> You twirl in an arc.
> But the falcon doesn't need
> Any German tricks,
> And the young man
> Holds them in contempt.

And this text, which I recorded myself in a partisan group during the war (verse by boys and girls driven out to Germany):

> GIVE AN ANSWER
> Ask a question, and answer,
> Dear daughters of the country,
> What can be fouler in this world
> Than what you're doing here.
> Meanwhile, all around, it's perishing,
> The fatherland . . .
> The people suffer impossibly,
> The country is perishing in blood,
> But for you—it's all the same to have some fun,
> Offer yourselves to Europe,
> Throw your heads down,
> Hugging an Italian with your arm.
> Or lie down with a Czech, in a roadside ditch—
> As if in your own marriage bed—
> And lose your Soviet pride,
> Everywhere, infinitely.

This was in Belarus, in the Sköpen area. There were a lot of little boys from partisan groups there—they were likely all thrown in jail later. And a major breakthrough to Minsk started there; Zhukov came to visit us.

And since it was clear that after the Spanish Civil War we too would have a great front, we experienced the war in Spain as directly as if it were our own. I remember the names of a hundred military posts and International Brigade battlefronts. I'll note parenthetically that by then we already knew Hemingway—we read and devoured his *A Farewell to Arms*—it was published in the journal which I think was still called *International Literature* at that point. We read like we were intoxicated. During my last two years of high school I finished Tolstoy and my father bought me the complete twelve-volume set of Dostoevsky. In our family, books were the only gifts children received, and money spent on books was never begrudged. I read as if possessed.

Bor'ka and I even tried to scramble through to the local seaport (where ships would depart for Spain) so we could climb into the hold as stowaways. But of course we were caught, and after we were subjected to a thorough interrogation (vigilance!) we were released peacefully. When I went into the army in 1940, Bor'ka wasn't accepted. He was going through a terrible love affair at the time. (His love interest, Zhenya Zenova, later married a man—and this is already a postwar recollection—who was apparently terribly jealous of her memories of the late Bor'ka, and apparently instilled in her a tendency towards anti-Semitic sentiments and speech, which were formerly totally foreign to her. Before the war, of course, nothing of the kind took place.[4])

Unexpectedly for me, I graduated high school with straight-As and a red certificate of excellence. I suspect that Efim Grigorievich may have touched up my final essay a little bit. I wrote the essay

---

4 I'll note in parentheses that I also really never ran into problems of this sort on the front. Sometimes I annoyed the people around me, just as any person does—for instance, with my lack of experience in physical labor. But I soon overcame this and handled physical labor easily; in particular, I got used to dragging heavy 160-millimeter shells. And shells, I'll note for the reader, are absolutely safe to drop on the ground; in order to make one live, you have to rotate it on an axis—then the detonating fuse passes into combat position. We would sometimes let heavy shells fall fuse-first onto rocks so that their fuses would be totally deformed. I do not recommend experiments of this nature to anyone. (For the curious: this is the case with shells, but not with mines.)

on Blok's *The Twelve*, using up an entire notebook, and I failed not only to re-copy the essay but even to edit it. There must have been significantly more mistakes than were listed: "0 orth. / 1 synt."—it was a rough draft! I'm sure that Efim Grigorievich indulged me a bit, as he often encouraged my literary interest and turned a blind eye to some of my orthographic deficiencies. And the grade was an "Excellent." This allowed me to receive my red certificate, which in turn allowed me to enroll at university without taking entrance exams. Whether it was the good heart of Efim Grigorievich or that some orthographic inspiration had dawned on me, it certainly played a big role: on graduation night I arrived without a jacket, and later we wandered through Leningrad all night, and I came down with terrible pneumonia and lay in bed until the beginning of September. If I'd had to take entrance exams, I wouldn't have been able to enroll at university at all that year and my fate would have taken a different path. By September I had recovered.

The time between the start of classes and the arrival of my army draft notice was, without any exaggeration, a truly happy time. Gukovsky taught Introduction to Literary Scholarship, and Introduction to Linguistics was taught by Aleksandr Pavlovich Riftin[5], a first-rate specialist in Semito-Hamitic philology. Both taught brilliantly. At university everything was as if in a fairy tale for me. I established a very good relationship with my class. It was a wonderful group, and although almost all the boys were soon drafted into the army, three boys remained behind—I wasn't of age yet, and got drafted a year later, in the beginning of my second year—and two others didn't go for health reasons, and both died later during the blockade.

In my first year I became taken with folklore. I took extra-curricular classes with Mark Konstantinovich Azadovsky and I gave a very successful presentation in Vladimir Yakovlevich Propp's seminar. (Propp's classes were always seminars; Azadovsky gave the lectures—they were both terribly interesting.) The presentation was on the

---

5 Riftin was the dean. He lead the department and preserved it during evacuation, restored it to Leningrad, and died on the very day that P. N. Berkov called him to say that the war was over. He just hung up, got up from the table, and died. He was a wonderful person and an outstanding scholar.

struggle between the father and the son in Russian folklore (with parallels in German folklore). I think Propp really liked it. At any rate, when I arrived back at university after the war, in a soldier's overcoat and German boots[6], I saw Propp in the hallway outside the dean's office and greeted him. He looked at me (I imagine that I didn't seem all that "martial" in my long overcoat, to use an expression of Peter the Great's) and greeted me and said, "Hang on, hang on. You're

---

6 They were distinctive in that their tops were in the shape of a truncated cylinder, widening towards the top (German soldiers stuffed the magazines for their machine guns into them), and I must have looked significantly less heroic with my skinny legs than I thought I did at the time. I didn't wear them out of a sense of fashion so much as out of necessity: I'd hopelessly grown out of all my pre-war clothes and shoes. I also went around in my uniform for the whole first year after the war; my soldier's shirt looked funny, weighed down by two orders and eight medals. But neither I nor anyone else found the question "How does it look?" interesting at that point—we were above such vulgarity. Girls who had come back from the army also went to lecture in Kirza boots and combat uniform (for instance, Lenina Ivanova, a wonderful girl who later married Vit'ka Maslov). Among the girls there was also another group, usually from wealthier, more professorial families, and we called them "dollies." They demonstrably rebelled against our asceticism (that is to say, they wore lipstick) and our "ideology" (that is to say, they went dancing). Their queen bee was Natasha, Gukovsky's daughter. She had a tragic fate, but after her father's arrest, this "dolly" proved herself to be a solid and courageous person. Later we became very close with her.

Natasha was a year ahead of me at school. When Gukovsky was arrested and his apartment was sealed shut (they left just one room for Natasha), and she was abandoned by the merry group of friends that had always flocked around her, and she was alone in this half-sealed-off apartment, expecting a child—she energetically fought for her father and constantly went to visit the investigation bureau. At that time she got married to Kostya, Arkady Semenovich Dolinin's son. On Dolinin's part, this was a gesture of nobility and bravery—his family opposed the marriage that obviously saved Natasha from exile. When I found out that her birthday was coming up, I saved all my money, bought a big bouquet of roses and a lovely little box of "Mareshal" candy, and dropped in on Natasha. We spent all day talking, almost until dusk, and we've remained friends to this very day—I would even say close friends.

(Yuri Mikhailovich didn't remember that significantly before this visit with Natasha Gukovskaya, he went to go see her family at what was for them a critical moment. In those anxious days, when Gukovsky was expecting to be arrested any minute, a decisive knock at the door made them all flinch; and suddenly a merry exclamation rang out from the open door: "It's Yura Lotman!" Natasha Gukovskaya-Dolinina recalled this episode later. [Lidiya Lotman's note])

Lida Lotman's brother. No, you yourself are Lotman." (This wasn't only to my credit, of course—Propp had a startling memory and apparently remembered the majority of his students.) Among the various prizes and encouragements given generously (and I fear not always deservedly) to me by life, I keep the words of Propp as one of the most precious.

In the very beginning of my second year I was summoned to the military enlistment office and informed that in the course of the next few weeks I would be drafted into the army. I hastened to take all my exams for the second year in advance (at the time this seemed incredibly foolish, but later, when I returned, it turned out to be very convenient, in a strange way).

At last I received my order to appear at the enlistment office. Everything seemed very simple and prosaic. Everyone knew that war was approaching, but somehow feverishly tried not to think about it. Everyone, at least everyone in my circle, continued to have fun, and the movie *If Tomorrow Brings War* (1938) came out in theaters, and everyone sang the song with the same name. The movie and the song were both quite cheerful:

If tomorrow brings war,
If the enemy attacks,
If he breaks out like a black storm cloud . . .

The gun carriages represented the principle striking force of the imminent war. The film ended with a celebration of victory after the war: popular actors watched us from the screen (of course none of them died in the war onscreen) while victory fireworks blazed behind them. This was how war seemed to us. Well, it was like this, but also not like this. We all read Remarque's *All Quiet on the Western Front* and Hemingway's *A Farewell to Arms* and heard and talked a great deal about world revolution, about the Second World War. And somehow we were diligently forgetting about it.

That feeling reminds me of the following experience, a personal one, from the summer of 1942 when we were breaking out of military encirclement. We were dragging the artillery guns, which were usually driven by tow-tractors, right along with us. In a few minutes—I can't say how long, maybe fifteen, maybe forty minutes—two tractor drivers were killed, and new ones were sitting in their places (the drivers couldn't pull over, and found themselves virtually without protection from their slow, six or eight kilometers per hour, awkward machines). They were civilian tractors, and we had earlier comandeered them from the kolkhoz. I remember that the same feeling of the approaching threat, and with it that desire to forget about it, stayed with us until the break. We all fell asleep feverishly, "to stock up" on sleep, feeling that this rest was necessary. It was the same before the war: although we didn't speak of it, we all felt that we would still need these minutes. Everyone was in a hurry to have fun.

It was also like that at home. My father left for a business trip the day before I had to appear at the enlistment office. I went out to a student party, which my class had organized as a farewell to me, and it so happened that I left for the army without saying goodbye to my father and never saw him again. My mother went to work at her clinic. The only one to see me off was my middle sister Lida, who brought me candy.

We were seen off solemnly. Before loading, we were arranged around the train cars and the commander of our eschelon announced that an old Petersburg proletarian would address us in a farewell speech. I have remembered this speech my whole life as though it were the Lord's Prayer: "Boys! I look at you and I'm sorry for you. But when I think about you, oh, I don't give a f***!" "To your compartments!" roared the commander, and we set out on a long journey.

We went merrily along in our heated freight car, and we got divided up into smaller groups. I was on the second level of the car, and the third level was taken by a group who called themselves the Lords, and their level was the Lords' Chamber. We, naturally, opposed them as a democracy.

The trip was great fun. Everything was new—both the lifestyle and the geography: we were being taken to Georgia. They only let us know where we would be serving once we got to Kutaisi. The 427th artillery regiment was assigned as our duty station. In this regiment (its name was changed: first it became a "guard regiment," and then a "brigade"), under Regiment Commander K. Dolst, I served through the entire war.

Dolst was German. It must be said that this particular nationality did not speak well of its bearer in such a situation, and he called himself Latvian, but everyone knew the truth. By this time most of the officers from middle- and high-ranking positions had been arrested, and the army had been virtually handed over to younger officers who now had positions above their rank. Ironically, this turned out to be quite advantageous, in the miltary sense: the old top-level command, from the times of Voroshilov and Budyonny, or the Arakcheev-types like Marshal Timoshenko, proved totally unfit for anything during wartime.

I did see Marshal Timoshenko once, and only once, when I had extended the phone lines into the headquarters of some very high-ranking staff—I don't remember which headquarters exactly. He was sitting in a trench shelter, three dirt-layers deep (our dugout was covered with fir branches, with earth sprinkled on top), and he was barely able to squeeze out a word for the trembling of his lips, although there was no sign of real danger around.

Although it seems wild to say it now, I daresay that the cruelty of the Stalinist terror that swept through the army had a positive side against all expectations, even those of Stalin himself: this terror purged the army of incompetent and uncultured commanders left over from the first post-revolutionary years. It is true that among the "repressed" there were courageous and talented people—their turn to die came first. But the terror was so vast that fools fell victim to it as well. At any rate (and here I will avoid general speculations and stick to speaking from personal experience), my regiment was manned by young commanders (the word "officer" wasn't being used at that point) who were well prepared, despite the fact that they were occupying positions higher than their ranks. As I spent the entire war with these commanders, I'll say a few words about them. Battery Commander Captain Grigoriev was a brilliant artilleryman. Our platoon commander, Shaliev, had been a reservist earlier and had just been called to service. We called him the Old Man—he was a little over forty. He was an intelligent man, and more importantly, very calm in combat conditions. He had no military bearing whatsoever, and he was a fantastic artilleryman. When the war ended he was no longer in our regiment: he was made a general, and I think he was killed at the end of the war.

For us, the beginning of military activity was long-awaited and therefore relieving. Besides, it was fun (yes, yes—fun!) to experience in practice what we had so long only experienced in our minds. I remember one of my first days: I'm in the line of fire at the telephone. Artillery is firing away. Despite the falling shells nearby, a one-and-a-half ton truck rolls right up to the guns. The battalion commander jumps down from the fender (it was considered especially cool to stand on the fender of the car instead of riding inside. Besides being cool, you could also see the diving planes more quickly. But being cool was important too) and swiftly, with a thundering, commanding voice, he utters, "Well done, First (that is, the First Battery—that was us)! You're getting shot at, and you're shooting back, and what do we get? An artillery duel."

The time that elapsed between my arrival at my unit and the beginning of the war was filled with the usual circumstances of soldierly training and does not deserve a detailed account. Only our trips for "combat firings" were new. The southern winter rains were endless; we dragged our tank guns along the mountains. Once one of them slid off the slippery mud covering the mountainside and dropped down. Fortunately no one was killed. It was later extracted by three tanks.

I was always wet and covered with mud, but I still took pleasure in my full freedom after months spent in the barracks.

The Georgian Highlanders were extremely friendly. When we were wet and muddy, they would often invite us to their cabins built from flat stones up on top of the low mountains; they warmed us, dried our clothes, and fed us. I remember that the owner of one house had been a soldier in the First World War, and he would recount his experiences at length, explaining to us what war is.

Soon after we returned from training, the order came that our regiment was to be split into two parts: one to remain in the Caucasus, the other to be transferred to the Western border. I soon found myself in a train compartment with the others who were to go West.

We were brought into Shepetovka, and soon moved to the camps in Yuzvin. War was clearly approaching—we could tell by how often they explained to us at political lectures that war between the USSR and Allied Germany could not be.

With war imminent, I had firmly decided to show that I wasn't a wimp, and so divided all of my free time between French books and the pull-up bar. By the time the war began, I had passed all the athletic tests (running and jumping have never been difficult for me, and I trained hard enough on the pull-up bar to earn myself a solid army "B").

So that was how the war began for me. Camp life was tent life. Behind the tents stretched one of our "lanes," a path for regiment soldiers that we used. In front of the tents was another "lane," only used by on-duty guards and officers who were on detail that day (it was strewn with some nice yellow sand). Further on was one more "lane," which nobody used. The guard was stationed there, and only those who swept and collected fallen leaves were permitted to step onto that path. The commanding general could take it, too, if he bothered to stop by our unit. One morning we headed off to training as usual; that is, we loaded ourselves up with coils, shovels, and axes—everything that had been set by the regulations—and we set off to the woods to sleep. By lunch we had slept our fill and began to march back in parade step, in cheerful song. But as we approached the camp, we suddenly saw that on the third "lane," our "holy of holies," a puffing tow-tractor had completely ploughed the road. It immediately became clear that nothing except the end of the world could have occurred in our absence. The camp was all upside down. Battle alarm was declared. Lined up in full marching order, we listened to the declaration (it was made by Commissar Rubenshtein; Dolst had left for staff headquarters to receive a military assignment) that we would soon depart, in exact accordance with the training plan, to a new stage of combat preparation (this was three days before the war, this was the 19th), and that this stage of instruction, which we had to undergo, was called "mobile camp": we would only move forward at night, whereas by day we would camoflage in the woods and roadside bushes. And then, his voice having changed somewhat, the commissar added: "Whoever smokes at night gets shot on the spot." After those words, further elucidation was unnecessary.

I remember perfectly the general feeling of joy and relief that had enveloped us (I write "us" because we would talk to each other about this), the kind of feeling you get when you have a molar pulled. As Pushkin's Salieri says:

As if I had accomplished a great duty,
As if a healing knife had severed from me
The suffering limb!

For us, the alliance with Hitler was something unnatural, a sense of danger in pitch darkness. And now it began, that very thing for which we had been preparing, that thing for which we were building ourselves: the war which we supposed would be the beginning of world revolution, or at least the continuation of the Spanish overture. I can't affirm that everyone around me felt exactly this feeling, but the feelings of the Leningrad youth, of my friends, were roughly the same. However, my friend Perevoshchikov[7] was smarter. When we would say, "Thank God the war's begun!" he would add, "Now both Stalin and Hitler will fly off . . ." (without specifying where). Others were of a different mind, although we didn't hide our thoughts from each other. In any case, the blister burst.

In helmets, in uniform jackets to match our heights, with tri-linear rifles (the automatics we could only see from afar—headquarters' chiefs carried them) we rode with pride (later, our movement sped up, and we were already moving day and night) through towns, and girls from bordering towns would pelt us with flowers and shout

---

7 Well before we began working on *Non-Memoirs*, during a regular conversation, when Yuri Mikhailovich was telling me about the time before the war and the feeling of those years, I wrote down some of his phrases about "Nikolka Perevoshchikov": that he "laughed at everyone, living his own experience as though it were someone else's," "was a defeatist, and expected war with America," "talked about everything with an ironic smirk." On the front, he once received a package with provisions from Leningrad during the blockade, and his family died of starvation soon after that. One younger sister survived, and Yuri Mikhailovich saw her in Leningrad after the war. (Jelena Pogosjan's note)

(this is exactly how it went): "Don't let any Germans near us!" Later, when it was time to "scram"—this was our technical term to designate a retreat—how shameful it was to remember those moments!

And especially shameful, I remember, was when we went out and walked through a large village, or little town—as ever, on both sides of the road stood crowds of women and children. And a boy saw my rifle and cried out, "That rifle is rusty!" I didn't sleep that night: I cleaned and oiled my rifle. After that—I flatter myself with hope—I never had a rusty rifle again.

Let me give another example, this time from the "scram" of 1942. We were walking through an abandoned military camp, and we collected some hand grenades and even some canned goods, left by those on the rear lines as they feverishly retreated, and my best friend Lyoshka Egorov[8] took the most absurd thing I ever saw during the war and pinned it to himself: a little front line flask, cast from glass by some kind of folks in the rear who were carrying out the plan. Carrying a glass flask in front line service is the height of absurdity. With astonishment I asked Lyoshka what the hell it was, and received in reply: "Scram or no scram, I'm keeping the look of a fighter in full uniform, so the locals can see that we're not scramming; we're retreating according to plan." And indeed he was not scramming, but retreating.

The beginning of the war caught up to us not far from the old border. In the middle of the night we approached the Dniester in the Mogilev-Podolsky area and immediately turned around. The

---

8 I have to mention this remarkable person—an authentically working-class guy (he was a metalworker), a poet, falling in love at every new place where we were stationed, with the most sublime, usually Platonic, love. I remember some verses he composed in '42 in the Caucasus:

Wherever you look—only mountains everywhere,
Wherever you look—the Caucasus region.
But among those mountains is the town
Where my darling lives.

I also remember a time in Ingushetia, a year later, when we were sleeping on the floor of a shed, and the owner's daughter was squatting in the doorway. Lyosha came in, and I accidentally overheard her words: "Everyone slept, me no sleeped, waited you."

observation point was on the old border, on the high bank of the Dniester. The line was seven kilometers long, divided in the middle by the interim point, and I was on that point. The front still hadn't reached the old border (the banks of the Dniester, where we had turned around). For three days we stayed there as though we were in the rear lines, without seeing any troops in front of us. Before us lay Moldavia, where our front troops must have been. I don't know whether they were really there, but no one from our troops came to us on that side. On the right, on the Kiev side, there was rumbling. Above us, German planes flew by intensely, but didn't bomb. The biggest event of those days was locating in the same area where our rear lines had just been. I don't know why the rear-line officers fled, and so chaotically, as if the retreat had been under direct pressure from the Germans, even though they were still quite far off. They had left behind all their belongings.

Climbing between the abandoned boxes of ammunition, shells, and weaponry, we discovered two big boxes of eggs (I don't know how many exactly, but there must have been several thousand). We communicated this "along the line," and people began to come to us from all points of the battalion. I remember that we ourselves ate scrambles made of four hundred eggs each after the rather meager military rations.

Now a small digression on military language. Military language is distinguished primarily in that it shifts the semantics of words. To use words in their regular sense is contrary to front line linguistic panache. This is not an individual act, but somehow dialects arise spontaneously, depending on the occurance of certain dominant words that are usually linked to the dominant elements of everyday life (and life develops very quickly, even mobile life, as during a retreat, for instance). In its nomenclature, this everyday life is very limited and common throughout the entire space of the front, so that the words from this life become a sort of sub-language. The defining word of 1941 through the summer of 1942 was "to steal." You can signify nearly everything with this word: "to steal" could mean "to rob," it could mean "to run off to some other activity," as in "to steal away to the women," and even "to fall asleep," ("while you were out walking, I stole an hour of sleep"), or "to evade the orders of one's superiors," etc. In general, it meant some kind of spirited action about which one could boast. I remember one furious officer from another unit who'd just gotten something nicked from his car, shouting at his driver, "While you were catching a snooze, someone stole off with my pistol and all my stuff!" There were other similar words, words by which we understood immediately whether a guy was from our front line or not—a kind of jargon.

The direct meanings of words were tabooed. So, for instance, there was a consistent taboo on the word "to rob." It seemed related to the other, insulting set of semantics—the civilian, the peacetime. We knew that the Germans employed the verb "to organize" in its stead, also refusing to use "to rob," also finding in it an unpleasant taste.

At some point in the novel *Under Fire*, Barbusse cited a conversation between a trench writer and some fellow soldiers. The soldiers were interested in how their front line comrades would describe the war—would they use expletives or not? And they firmly assured him that to write truthfully about war without expletives was impossible. From my own experience I will say that the matter at hand does not only concern the need to convey the truth. Sophisticated, well-selected profanity is one of the most important means to adapt to the most difficult conditions. It bears indisputable features of art and brings a playful element to everyday life, which, psychologically, considerably eases the experience of supremely difficult circumstances.

Everyone's mood was feverishly cheerful. The soon-to-be totally useless forty-fives (45 mm or anti-tank guns) would drive past us to the very front lines. The commander of one of these little guns was a dashing, handsome Georgian all decked out in badges won in army competitions. He would stop by and have a smoke with us. I remember how suavely and grandly he held his German cigar (which was so cool that he didn't even inhale, so as to stretch it out a little longer). He informed us of how many shots he could make in a minute, and added, "I'll burn seven tanks before they crush me!" (This formula didn't sound buffoonish; it sounded natural. That was how we calculated.) That same night I met him again. He was dirty, in a torn uniform shirt, and there was no gun nearby. "You know, Yurka," (we already addressed each other informally) he literally sobbed, rather than said, "our guns just can't get those tanks. I hit the tank eight times, but (and here let us alter his vocabulary) it doesn't give a damn." His own little gun was crushed.

We spent two full days under continuous fire, and kept to the original position. The observation post was already occupied, and the scouts and operators, along with the battery commander, ran over to us in the line of fire. We held on to that line for another half day. Towards evening on the second day of our war, we were ordered to retreat four hundred meters at nightfall. Incidentally, when night fell, the field kitchen indulged us: instead of our evening gruel we got excellent rice cereal—a reserve we hadn't been allowed to consume. Our general mood was, as the soldier's saying goes, "Once the booze has gone this far, better slice the last pickle!" With that, the retreat began, and at first, it was fairly well-organized.

Taking advantage of the fact that the enemy did not fight at night, and that with the setting of the sun all combat would cease, we held fast to one principle: withstand until sunset. When the southern dark night came on, we would quickly wind up the lines and fall back, at first for only a few kilometers. There we would spread out and dig trenches, and in the morning it would all start over again. But after a few days the "Junkers" intensely bombed a small station of ours in the rear lines, and early in the morning, tanks burst through from somewhere to that side. It was our first encirclement. After that the word "encirclement" became one of our most commonly used words.

Factually, one couldn't call it encirclement, just as a layered cake can't be called a pretzel. It was a shifting state of armies entangled amongst each other, and these armies were always striving to form something that could be called by a name from a military textbook: "the front." Gradually, a different principle, one unforeseen by military theory, began to dominate: those who possessed the greater speed of movement often found themselves ahead (so, for example, the headquarters, automobile convoys, supplies, and tanks ended up furthest from everyone, at the rear), often entirely losing touch with the other scattered units in combat. And the infantry and artillery were left behind.

We had excellent guns and very good artillerymen, but we lost our assigned high-speed tow-tractors fairly soon. And then we weren't given anything to replace them until 1943. We used agricultural crawler tractors comandeered from various kolkhozes, which could go six kilometers an hour, which is to say they had exactly no hope of getting away from the enemy. It is precisely because of this that our heavy artillery bore such bad equipment losses. Anyway, we somehow dragged our tank guns with us; we didn't drop them. We figured out how to connect two three-ton trucks to the guns. On level ground and even uphill the things went just fine. But the tank guns rumbling down the mountain put pressure on the rear of the trucks and the drivers ran beside their trucks in terror, driving by hand or standing on the fender. Then the rain started. The enemy equipment began to sink into the sticky, wet, black earth, and front line movement slowed. Wet, sinking into the liquid black earth, we cursed the rain, which in fact had helped us a great deal.

In the beginning of the war they began to give out the famous front line hundred grams, that is, one hundred grams of vodka (I should note that later, during retreats and encirclements, there were shortages of food, we didn't receive our mail for months, and ammunition was delivered to us with only relative regularly, but we received Stalin's hundred grams consistently, without interruption). Of course, on their way to us they got sipped from a lot, but the losses in vodka were covered by our losses in men, so that the hundred grams generally reached us in full and undiluted.

Before the war I wouldn't even sniff vodka. We had wine with dinner at home (my father knew wines and liked good ones), but vodka would appear only on holidays for guests. When they began to give out vodka as part of our ration, I gave my portion to the other boys for the first two days. But then five of my friends gathered up and poured all their daily rations together. In one breath I dashingly drank down half a liter of vodka. I only remember that I managed to crawl into the trench and fell fast asleep on some straw.

I don't know how much time passed, but I was shaken awake. While I rubbed my eyes, the boys yelled into my ears that the Germans had broken through the front to the west of us and they had

gotten deep into the rear lines, and that we were virtually in encirclement again and had to immediately wind up. "Wind up" in this case
had two meanings: "wind up the fishing rod," which meant "let's
scram," or wind up the coils of telephone cord. In case of a retreat
these two meanings merged. I was shaken awake, and I found the
strength to accomplish my work—I wound up my coils and began to
drag them off. Not without pride I will say that I delivered the coils
and the apparatus to their place in one piece. But then the boys began
to tell me how, contrary to orders to move silently and speak only in
a whisper, I had shouted satirical verse along the whole road, which
we at the front had picked up from various theatrical actors. Thus the
comical "Fritz" was given these lyrics, which we turned into our own
ironic hymn:

> Now I'm just a bumpkin who don't give a damn,
> But I always know when it's time to scram . . .

The war consisted in the daily work of our battery, and then
later a quick wind up and nightly retreat in order to deploy to a new
place before dawn, restore all lines of communication, and then at
dawn begin work again. This lasted until the winter. In December
unexpectedly strong frosts came along (in general, the war years
were marked by exceptionally harsh winters—harsher, according to
the locals, than they had been for a long time). For me, the war is
somehow inextricably linked to rainy autumn, to guns and trucks,
sunk to the axles in the black earth, and our endlessly dragging them
out, and those harsh winter frosts.

In general (and this feeling is not mine alone; I have consulted
others), our basic internal state was the desire "for it to just go to hell
and be done with already!"—a thirst for the end. In winter you wait
for the frosts to end, you rub your ears, you stop up your cracked
boots (in 1943 they gave us American boots—they were like iron, we
couldn't wear them out before the war ended, they ground our feet
'til we bled), but the German tanks and planes, running on their artificial gasoline, could not withstand our frosts. The summer is warm,
it's sheer bliss, you can change your clothes, and beat your lice, snatch

some time to rest, and most importantly—you don't freeze. You don't even have to sleep in your hut, but anywhere, even on a haystack. But from morning until night the "Junkers" (87 and 88) are crawling across the sky. It becomes clear that the enemy has better tanks, and soldiers swear at the clear sky and good weather with all their strength. They wait for autumn and winter, only to rub their hands and dance to warm their feet, only to curse the winter. During the winter of 1942, our station was called the "Pine tree." I remember the constant question all through the line: "Pine tree, pine tree, will the second spring come soon?" Days we wait for night, nights we wait for day. In the summer we wait for winter, and winter for summer. That's the law of the front.

There is a bright side. It's not as scary on the front as it seems when you describe it or read about it in books. The best way to get rid of fear is generally to plunge into whatever causes it. If you're afraid of the front lines, then, in order to get rid of your torment, go to the front. We were all terrorized by the constant threat of encirclement. But hardly anyone would believe what relief enfolds you when something really happens—when, instead of waiting and feeling, you have to act. And encirclements aren't as frightening as the wait for them or the stories about them. Even war isn't as frightening as when you're waiting or remembering it from a distance. Diving into it is the best remedy for fear. I often had to deal with people who, having seized onto the nearby rear lines or headquarters, would become pathologically cowardly, and would wound themselves, which would mean execution by firing squad, so as not to end up at the front. But I am absolutely sure that they were regular people, and not at all abnormally cowardly in their regular lives. And if fate had dropped them into real trouble from the beginning, had introduced them to the war before they managed to "spook," then they would never have gotten "sick." I write that they got "sick" because it's a real sickness; I've seen many people who really are sick with it. You've got to jump right into cold water, rather than deliberating on the shore.

The other boys and I were very lucky in that we ended up where it seemed most frightening in our very first days. And we ascertained that the fear was essentially determined by our imaginations, and by the relation between reality and habit. Later, when I was already an experienced sergeant, and we began to receive "young'uns" from the rear lines (this was already at the end of the war), I would regularly take one of them and walk him over to where it seemed the least pleasant to be. This was necessary in order to convince a person that fear is born not from objective conditions (that is, from the size of the danger), but from our relations to them. (By the way, horror movies beautifully demonstrate this. If cheap flicks can generate fear in the viewer with monstrous film shots, then Hitchcock brilliantly showed that any safe object from everyday life can also be filmed such that the viewer finds himself on the verge of a heart attack from terror.)

We retreated to the Don River (this was the summer of 1942). The Germans didn't move at night; we made use of this, and in the night we managed to slip away from the German front line units by about 30 kilometers on foot, even though they were moving along on motorcycles and armored tanks.

Your feet get absolutely wrecked. And when you get up after a short rest, it seems it'd be easier to kick the bucket than take one more step. But the boys are already walking off. So you force yourself to take the first, second, third step—and they hurt. Your soles are ravaged, and your toes. You can't straighten your legs. And everyone's taking their first steps like this, and when you look around at the others, you might die of laughter. Your ravaged footrags stick to your feet and that hurts a lot. We generally stopped taking off our shoes. Because it was clear that putting them back on again would be impossible and then we'd have to go barefoot. And you don't walk far when you're barefoot. So you manage the first kilometer, and then your feet get used to it, your footrags somehow fit more softly in your boots. First hour—short break—second hour . . . and towards morning, look, we just covered about 30 kilometers.

Once in a while a "frame" flies over us—a German reconnaissance twin-engine "Heinkel" aircraft, which gets its name from the forked fuselage between its wings and tail. It circles us and flies off. We quip, "Well, it got a nice picture of us, we should order a print to send home," or even, "Now at German headquarters they're all gonna notice we haven't shaved today." We all shoot at the "frame" together, but it doesn't pay any attention to us. After it's gone we wait for the "Junkers." That's how it always goes. First we hear a buzzing, and then bombers appear—not a whole lot, usually three, sometimes six, depending on whether we're in a little group or a crowd. There's the "Junkers 87"—a single-engine diver plane, a good one, and it dives straight down with a horrible roar and very accurately drops bombs (which doesn't make us happy at all).

Still from a distance, though they've obviously already seen us, already decided that we're a goal worthy of attention—the "Junkers," in triangular formation, stretch out onto the line. Later, they enact their well-known, rigorously ritualized procedure, which is very similar to the behavior of prey animals or insects. While the "Junkers" fly in a triangle, we can stay calm, and they head somewhere else. But look, they've stretched out in a zigzag, they're dropping back in a circle whose center is just a little ahead of us. Which means they're going to pay us a visit. We run down from the road in all directions and press ourselves to the earth. The earth is our primary defense. And the "Junkers," in a zigzag, head towards us. Now the first one dispatched, sharply turned with his nose to the earth, almost vertically, with all the beauty of an exact calculation, falls on us. The bombs detach from it—we see them very well. It seems they're falling right onto your head. The bombs overtake the plane. Around you, you can hear muffled eruptions; the earth trembles. The pilots dive artistically, swinging almost to the ground—ours never dive like that. The plane is like a hypnotist—attracts your gaze and nothing can tear it away. That's probably how a rabbit would write about a rendezvous with a cobra.

From the layers of smoke and dust covering the earth, reaching the limit with a howl, the plane breaks away, straight up. As it rises, it still manages to splash us with machine gun fire or fire from the air gun. But the whistle of the bullets isn't audible, because the next one is howling as it falls. In these moments you shut off, you don't experience that feeling of fear, you don't experience any feelings at all—you probably feel like the stones lying beneath us. Finally the last plane has dropped its bombs, and they fly off. We get up.

I was always surprised at the low efficiency of these raids. Of course, on dense masses of infantry, or on moving armored vehicles, or on deployed guns or tanks, these air strikes were very effective.

But on scattered and retreating army units, whose soldiers had time to jump into a ditch or drop into some shelter, the strikes weren't all that effectual. The smoke clears. To encourage ourselves, and to show the Germans that we're to be reckoned with, we manage to shoot at the plane a few times with a rifle. There were a hell of a lot of cartridges, they were scattered everywhere, and there was no need to conserve them. But I never saw any result from my daring. Either I had poorly calculated the forestalling, which at such low altitude must be very great, or the "Junkers" armor was strong, but I didn't make any trouble for the German Wehrmacht with those shots. Maybe somewhere on some wing I left a scratch, but I never managed a spectacular fall like the one described by Tvardovsky in *Vasily Tyorkin*, for instance, when the hero knocks out a twin-engine "Junkers". But the sense of this shooting was different: it really raises your spirits, you stop feeling like a rabbit, you can vent your energy. All in all, it's a good thing.

We're moving on to the Don. Because of the bombings and the German tanks that appear periodically, we have split up and are heading east in small groups—of maybe two or three men. We try to go with our own, from our own regiments, but we've practically all lost one another. In the steppes during the bombings I met a soldier from another battalion in our regiment, a Don Cossack. He soon found an exhausted horse in the steppes that had been abandoned by someone, and he mounted her. The horse, like me, could barely move her legs, and she and I went along on foot, with him astride. All along the way we discussed why the war was turning out so badly for us. My companion expressed his thought approximately with the following words: "Now don't you get angry, Yurka, but the Jews are to blame here. No, don't worry, I'm not saying it in a fascist vein, and you know I don't have those prejudices, but judge for yourself. Look, the Germans were preparing for the war, and we what—we were having festivals, and releasing the best films in the world, and Oistrakh was sawing on the fiddle—and they're all Jews. No, you know, I don't have any biases, I'm just saying we shouldn't have been playing the fiddle." I didn't share his views and I tried to explain to him that there was a war between fascism and anti-fascism, and that anti-fascism presumed a renaissance—the development of art. To which he replied, "Well, with all this renaissancing, there are Germans on the Don—so screw your renaissance!" But in general, we were moving along like friends. We separated only when we reached the Don in the dark southern night.

The darkness only thickened from the barges, vehicles, and all kinds of rubbish burning on the riverbanks—stuff the army had brought as far as the Don and then dropped there. We got to the riverbank, and we had to decide what to do next, as there was no crossing, and some confused detached soldiers were walking along the banks. A soldier who was running by said that we weren't far from a half-sunken barge where there was sugar and vodka, and the boys were drinking there like ants. My partner said that he would go and drink and bring something to drink back with him. I decided to cross the river while it was still dark.

How I was to do it, though, was totally unclear to me—I couldn't swim then and still can't today[9]. Stepping along the marshy sand on the very banks of the Don, I saw two black figures in coats that obscured their badges of rank (though they were commanders' coats) and I heard a fragment of conversation: they were talking about how they had to get a bunch of horses across the Don. One of the speakers was reporting that he'd found a strong boat and a guy who had some boat experience: he would hold a horse by the bridle, and it would swim, and they only had to find an experienced rower. I was seized by a wave of audacity. I came out of the darkness and approached them with the words, "Need a rower? Here I am." It seems my appearance did not inspire much confidence in the higher-ranking officer. "Look," he said, and then added a few words of military eloquence for persuasion's sake, "you'll drown yourself, but as for me . . . I don't care, just don't sink my horses." But I was already carried away. I said, "Don't scare me, it's just business as usual, I grew up near the sea . . ." We set off. I was at the oars; the other soldier took a horse by the bridle and sat in

---

9 Here—as in many other places—we see a self-disparagement typical of our author. In the sense of swimming laps, he could swim well enough, although, never having specifically learned the art of swimming, he did not know any strokes, and thus swam "barrel-style," as he called it. (Mikhail Lotman's note)

the stern; we pushed the boat off; the horse, bucking, lunged into the water, and I began to row. At first I was spinning—one arm racing the other—I was a good-for-nothing rower. But gradually I began to get the hang of it. The horse, trying to climb into the boat, got it good on the nose and began to swim. The second time was easier. I don't know how many times I made the trip, but finally I said, "I'm done for, boys, I'll take one more across and then I'm done, find someone else."

We went across. I crawled out of the boat and started off with a sense of having passed all limits of fatigue, expecting to run into our solid defense here on the riverbank. There I would receive further information about our itinerary. But there was no defense. Along this bank, too, detached soldiers were wandering around, just they were on the other side. Which way I was supposed to go was entirely unclear. I lay down on the wet river sand and it seemed like I was asleep before I could rest my head. I don't know how long I slept. Later, I stood and set off for the east, hoping that I would run into some kind of defense. It just couldn't be that our front was totally bare.

In that area the Don flows with multiple currents: some merging, some diverging. I didn't have the strength to look for a place to cross. I waded straight in, negotiating one deep parallel river arm after the other. The place was entirely deserted. I had absolutely no strength, but I found a way to sustain it: I walked and fired tracer bullets into the sky, one after another. In some strange way, this helped to overcome the feeling of being lost. All the while, I was wildly shouting the most unprintable expletives at the top of my lungs. The mix of shots and my wild swearing strangely sustained me. Finally, I crossed the last tributary, plunked myself onto the earth and immediately fell asleep again. Crossing the Don had been completed.

In the summer of 1942 the front became relatively stable. We were replenished and sent to the Mozdok area (Chechnya-Ingushetia). Malgobek, a little town located right on the Terek river, stood directly on the front lines. On the other side of the river, with the Cossack population, lay the first line of German defense. We held down the south bank, although the phrase "held down" here can only be used metaphorically: we had virtually no infantry. Our tank guns, to the extent that our limited supply of ammunition permitted, had to simultaneously perform their primary task—suppressing the enemy's artillery—and secure our crossing, to which they were ill-suited.

In the Ingushetian houses along the banks (the inhabitants had fled to the mountains, and the town was totally empty), we established a PFO (point of front line observation) and waited day after day for the start of a new wave of the German offensive. Using colorful soldier language, we discussed what we would do, given that we only had five rounds of ammunition. The enemy apparently did not even suspect how scarce our means were, and were actively accumulating reserves (we could see this perfectly), preparing for the breakthrough. It apparently hadn't crossed their minds that their opposition on this side consisted in an artillery detachment with virtually no ammunition, one mortar battery, and some miserable, quickly assembled and poorly equipped troops made up of the motliest crew, including cooks and clerks from headquarters. When I—not without irony—asked the upper lieutenant, "And what branch of combat are these?" he replied with the ornate profanity of an experienced front-liner, and we both burst out laughing.

The German observation point and headquarters were located right across from us on the opposite bank. We could see everything that was happening over there perfectly, and we could count on one hand the motorcycles which constantly rolled up and back. There was some lively staff-and-observation work going on over there, but we had so little ammunition that we were strictly ordered not to shoot unless the enemy began to cross. And our silence inspired the other shore.

One day (the weather was already really hot at this point) we saw that the guard on duty at the entrance to the headquarters was standing at his post completely naked, naked as the day he was born, only wearing boots and a machine gun around his neck. Not only was he thus shielded against the heat, but it was clear that he also took pleasure in the impression his appearance must be making on us. Standing and facing our post full-frontal, he chuckled and clapped himself on the belly. Our lieutenant couldn't bear such humiliation and asked headquarters for three rounds: "Come on, just to scare the pants onto him," he entreated the battalion commander, and received in reply: "Well, alright, let him have three pieces." It's almost impossible to adjust a gun in three rounds—even if you've already been shooting—and then there's the wind, and then the gun sinks with every shot, imperceptibly, but it does sink, especially in soft riverbank soil. All this can be disregarded during regular mass fire. It just wouldn't be noticeable. But this work was intricate and demanded utmost accuracy. Of course our gun fired three rounds without bringing any harm to our neighbor on the other bank. But he took the hint and put on some pants.

In general, our attitude towards the naked body was totally different than it was in the German army. This was clearly affected by the differences between European and Eastern views on the matter. The Germans not only weren't ashamed of unbuttonedness and the naked body (and these observations were made from across the front lines, so my opinion might need to be verified), but they even seemed to find it especially stylish. They would willingly drive around the front, naked on motorcycles, and in German war posters the front line German officer is always represented in a uniform unbuttoned to the chest and with rolled-up sleeves (in the German army this is all probably considered "Martial Chic"). But we were all accustomed to being prudish about our bodies (I don't remember any one of us, but especially the peasant boys, ever stripping to sunbathe). If we allowed ourselves this liberty in the heat during work, it might be that we would go naked from the waist up, but still in mandatory pants and boots.

However, I will note that in the winter we always wore hats, and the European style—to go without a hat in the cold—was totally unfamiliar to us. Many years later (this was in Norway), I inquired of my friend, not a young man at this point, who was walking around in the cold with a bare head, whether he wasn't cold without a hat, and received in reply, "But it makes one look so much younger!" Incidentally, I will note that in Russia, on the other hand, it is in style for little boys to cover their heads in the heat, but the opposite makes one appear more grown-up. The value may vary, but the place of head attire in the semiotics of age remains constant.

II. How to Remove Lice

THERE'S A SCENE in Tvardovsky's *Vasily Tyorkin* where an old man, a veteran of the First World War, is talking with Tyorkin and asks him: "But tell me just one thing, Do you guys have it?" "Have what?" "Lice."

To which Tyorkin replies with dignity, "Yes, partially." And the World War I veteran tells Tyorkin that this makes him a real soldier. No one who has written relatively truthfully about war, from Barbusse to Hašek[10], has avoided this topic. In part, lice is an illicit topic; it treats "that" side of life during wartime. Before the war I only knew about lice from literary classics or from my entomological research.

We moved on—it was the second month of the war, but the southern front was already quite hot. One day I felt a totally incomprehensible irritating itch. We were in the forest plantations in the steppes, waiting for night to fall so we could come out from hiding in the aircraft and start retreating again to the south. I slipped off a little further into the forest, threw off my shirt, and shuddered with disgust.

Entomology has always been an object of love for me, and this feeling has stayed with me even after I abandoned the idea of becoming a scholar of insects. Orthoptera and Neuroptera especially interest me, but it was on Coleoptera that I had been planning to write a study, and to this day I am sorry not to have written it. But I had some kind of physiological disgust for parasites, and especially for lice. When I saw a large white louse on my shirt, I shuddered—in the literal, unmetaphoric sense of the word—and barely kept from vomiting. I acted decisively and in accordance with the situation. I built a fire, set up a bucket of water over it, stripped naked and crammed everything except my boots and my papers into

---

10 See Hašek's *The Good Soldier Švejk:*

> The whole front has lice. They scratch furiously:
> Now the lower ranks, now the company commander.
> The general himself writhes against the lice like a lion,
> And tears off his uniform in less than a minute.

the bucket. Fortunately this soup had time to boil up nicely before we were called to march. I quickly wrung it all out, and, soaked to the threads, set off to catch up with the platoon. That was my first impression of lice.

However, the sharpness of that impression soon dulled, and we had to reconcile the constant appearance of the lice with the constant struggle against them. Fortunately, at the end of 1941, or the beginning of 1942 (I don't remember exactly), we found the right solution.

The Germans were also suffering from lice and fought them by sprinkling themselves with various chemical powders. But these products were not very effective. These insects were apparently entirely unknown to the enemy in their normal everyday lives, and so they were unable to find a working solution until the end of the war. As a result, we never stayed in German trenches when it came time to be on the offensive, even when we needed shelter from fire or frost: to climb into one always meant to collect insects. Our infantry, which naturally failed to set up even the most elementary liceproofing at the front, also suffered a lot from lice. But the artillery and the infantry of the second line had practically gotten rid of them by 1942. I don't know who he was, this genius who invented a simple and surefire solution, but I would build him a monument (I write this without any irony).

This was the solution. Finding an iron barrel on the front, the kind used for fuel, never presented any difficulty. They'd be lying near the broken, scorched machinery and other front line trash. There were tons of them. We'd construct the most elementary structure from these: we'd take the barrel and burn or wash out any remaining contents (gasoline, lubricating oil, fuel). After that, we carefully knocked out one of the ends, keeping the iron base intact. Then we would cut out two pieces of wood exactly as long as the diameter of the barrel, and hammer them on in a cross, at such a height that the uniforms hung on them wouldn't touch the bottom of the barrel. After that, the clothes in need of disinfestation were hung on the resulting cross. A little water was poured in and an iron lid, with a military overcoat wound around it for durability, was fitted to the top. Next the barrel was set up on some rocks and underneath it we would build a fire. In half an hour or maybe a little longer, the scorching barrel was opened. Pressurized steam would issue from it, and our laundry hung on the crosspiece, hot and sometimes glowing slightly if it touched the walls. No louse could withstand this experiment. It was very nice to wear squeaky-hot underwear. True, it was impossible to wash off the burnt mud, but that didn't bother us at all. The barrels were our salvation.

Not only did the lice naturally enter our lifestyle, but they also found their way into the folklore of the front. They were the topic of unceasing jokes and subtle, sophisticated swearing. They became the heroes of many incidents. Here's one of them.

In our battery, the commander of platoon control was an engineer from the Donets Basin, a sweet and intelligent man named Ivashchenko (the firing squad also had an Ivashchenko—also a lieutenant, and really insufferable). Ivashchenko went straight into the army from civilian life during a retreat and retained many civilian traits, but he was an excellent artilleryman, and a cheerful, amiable guy. Here's the story of what happened to him, which, speaking of lice, we would do well to remember.

This was in 1943, in the northern Donets Basin. The front was relatively calm, the observation post was maybe two kilometers away from the front line, and we decided to take advantage of these conditions to get rid of our lice. To do this, everyone on our side of the observation post, which was concealed from the front by the wall of a burnt house, set up a "barrel." The first to hang up his shirt, pants, and underwear was the battery commander, and when the contents were scorched through, Platoon Commander Ivashchenko hung his goods in the barrel. He wasn't used to it, since he was urban and cultured, and he really abhorred the lice. He stripped naked and hung everything in the barrel, leaving only his boots, and shouted at us, "Fire 'em, bastards, fire away!" We scorched the barrel. But the sparks must have risen too high, and suddenly, not too far off, first one shell fell, then another—the Germans were apparently adjusting their ranges—and then they began firing fairly thickly. We crawled into the trench. Poor Ivashchenko climbed in as he was—naked as the day he was born, in boots and clutching his party card, which he'd thought to take out of his pocket. He did not look very solemn, and we did not hesitate to poke fun at our commander's situation. When the fire ceased and it was safe to climb out, Ivashchenko rushed to the barrel: alas, everything was burnt. At the bottom of the barrel lay only a melted guard's badge, which the lieutenant had forgotten to unpin. Ivashchenko sat in his boots, naked, with his party card and his guard's badge in his hands, and viciously cursed the Germans, the war, and us—who, he supposed, had improperly hung up his clothes.

A call was placed to the battery to rush order underwear, pants, and the rest of the uniform for the lieutenant. But when the news spread along the line that observation post needed new underpants for Ivashchenko, a whole new wave of soldiers' jokes began. To his credit, it must be said that when his uniform was finally delivered, and with it came a bottle of vodka from the sergeant major, the lieutenant's mood lifted and he loudly expressed his joy that his Order of the Red Star had not been burnt.

This incident is worth recording, because there were always a lot of funny and jolly times during the hardest conditions. I would say that we laughed more at war than we later did during our peacetime lives, such as when the university was destroyed during the era of anti-cosmopolitanism.

III.

EARLY IN THE spring of 1944, our front lines were in Western Ukraine, and penetrated the enemy's lines in a long, narrow wedge formation. On our part, it formed a kind of tongue, about twenty kilometers long, and two hundred meters to a kilometer wide. The observation post was set up at the very tip, and the guns were located at the base. The enemy was firing at us from three sides, and there was practically nowhere in our area that was not under fire. I should add that the early spring had melted the snow, but the soil had thawed only in some places, so walking meant wading through water sometimes ankle-deep, sometimes knee-deep, slipping on the ice under the water, or sinking into a sticky mass of black earth. With each foot we pulled pounds of the liquid black sticky mass from the earth. It was absolutely impossible to run on that kind of terrain, and walking was exceptionally difficult. And we signalmen had to walk continuously. Fairly dense enemy fire continued in the area; pillars of water and mud and chunks of ice soared on all sides; our wet coats hung heavily from our shoulders; and our bestial faces were so dirty that we couldn't look at each other without laughing.

I walked along the line, which was crossed with shell splinters that had moved through this soup of earth, water, and ice, and had fallen under the thick, concentrated fire. I don't remember what words I used to express my feelings, but I can imagine that it was the lexicon referred to by linguists as expressive. I lay in the mud on a log. Shell splinters and clods of wet mud splashed down all around.

At this point a big hare, all splattered with mud, came running straight towards me through the water and mud, raising fountains as it ran. He was as unlucky as I was: he'd turn to the left—and a mine would fall to the left; he'd turn to the other side—and an accursed mine would fall there as well. Apparently entirely stupefied, spraying water and mud, he ran straight towards me and stood, nearly resting his nose against mine (it really may be that my eyes were squinting like his). We stared at each other in bewilderment.

I remember being struck by the thought that the hare was obviously thinking the same thing that I was: "What a mountain of iron, and all sent here with the sole purpose of killing me dead!" This same thought flashed through my mind with a tinge of pride—though whether the hare experienced pride, I cannot say.

One mine fell right near us and totally buried us in water and mud. The hare, who had apparently decided that it was too much already, raced across the water to the side. I thought that he was probably right and that it was better to abandon this place, because the enemy had apparently taken a liking to it. It was impossible to run, so I began to plod. Turning by chance, I saw that the hare was also plodding, but at a skip, tugging his legs from the mud with difficulty (I don't think any zoologist has ever seen a hare in such a state). I winked at him and it seemed to me that he smiled. We never met again.

IV.

IT IS HARDLY worth describing the events of the war in detail, week after week, month after month. They interest me because they concern me. They have no historical value—not because historical value is produced by "great people" participating in events, but because historical value is produced by the literary talent of the one doing the describing. Tolstoy wrote that, when a destitute musician in the Swiss city of Lucerne played for half an hour for the rich Englishmen listening to him and did not receive a penny from a single one of them, that was an incident worth including on the list of the events of world history. So the greatness of an event is derived from what happened, from the ability of the observer to interpret and pass on the event, and from the cultural code which is used by the one receiving the information. Since I do not possess the necessary ability to demonstrate the way a given event participates in history, further stories about the war can cease here.

Writing about war is hard, because only those who have never been to war know what it is. It's like describing an enormous space with no precise boundaries and no internal unity. There's one war in the winter, and another in the spring. One during a retreat, and another during defense and offense; one in the day, another at night. One in the infantry, another in the artillery, a third in aviation. One for the soldier, another for the journalist who's come to the front.

A journalist can spend many days in the war, can be on the front lines or in the rear lines of the enemy, can display great bravery and *live just like*—but he'll still have a completely different war. Because in the end he's sure to leave. He's on the front temporarily. A soldier is on the front permanently. I know the war from personal experience in the following guises: in 1941 and 1942 on the southern front, in 1943 on the southern and south-western, then on the western, and then on the Baltic front during the offensive, in Poland and in Germany. At first, in the very first days, we were on the Dniester, and from there we traveled on foot. Our battery truck was burned up in the very first weeks of the war, and later we would occasionally carry off any trucks we came across, but we'd soon lose them. In any case, the battery telephonist—and I was one—always walked. While he unwinds or winds up his coils, the trucks and tanks have time to advance in the event of an attack, or, less pleasant, move back in case of a "scram." After he's loaded himself up with the coils and apparatus (we usually carried two coils at about eight kilograms each), the telephonist walks on foot, catches up to the others, and finally finds his men in the mess that formed during the night movement of the army.

Our 437th artillery regiment with Commander Lieutenant Colonel Dolst was considered a shock regiment, and we were famous all along the front, but for us it just turned out to mean that we were always used to fill in gaps. This led to a constant back-and-forth from place to place and even from front to front—that is, it led to extra hardships.

Front life is significantly easier when the situation stabilizes and life takes on a more familiar form. Of course, in these conditions, bombings and shootings also occur regularly, and we run around on the line connecting cables, we collapse on the ice and experience all the other front line pleasures. But it's still regular life: you know where you can go warm up, and if you're on the firing line you know when the field kitchen will show up—or else an envoy heads to the kitchen with a thermos and brings back lunch, maybe cold, but lunch.

Life is totally different during a move. Retreat and attack have entirely different hardships. Retreat is incomparably worse than attack, but the losses are incomparably fewer. To be more precise, they are different in nature. Under retreat the whole division can get lost. We ourselves would repeatedly get lost—sometimes the whole regiment, the battery, and even individual men. Night scrams are tormenting with their incoherence, chaos, unexpected run-ins with the enemy, unexpected losses, lack of understanding of what to do, and complete ignorance of the situation.

Attack usually happens under conditions of less confusion, although there's still plenty of incoherence here as well. Collisions with the enemy generally happen during the day. But the losses suffered under attack are significantly greater. We never really knew how to attack and we never really learned. In the last months of the war, when it should have been easier (and by then the Germans weren't as bad—although their aviation continued to dominate in the air, it wasn't as strong as before, maybe three or nine planes), we continued to bear terrible losses, and the main thing was, it was all because of our own foolishness.

Dolst was a good artilleryman and preferred to shoot from the firing line, instead of shooting with direct fire. In the summer of 1943, pulling heavy guns into position for direct fire came into what might be called fashion among the commanders. In part this was necessary in order to break through the heavily reinforced, armored, multi-stage German line of defense. But there was another side to this trend: the pursuit of medals and awards had developed among those in command of the division and army. And this pursuit required, on the part of the commander, both showy breakthroughs and a tendency against saving his men—a tendency entirely alien to the units who had lived through the great retreat of 1941-1942 themselves. Losses were quickly replenished by new units from the rear, by young soldiers. Sheer quantity and huge sacrifices quickly compensated for the poor training of these replenished regiments. The commanders' pursuit of impressive phrases in war reports prompted these terrible, obviously unnecessary losses.

Such was the spirit of our new brigade commander, Ponomarenko. During attack he would sit in the trench with the army artillery chief and some kind of writer, who was apparently taking delight in experiencing front line danger. Ponomarenko had a German vodka decanter with a little glass rooster affixed to the bottom. They invented a game involving this rooster: "drown the cock" (fill the bottle of vodka), "save the cock" (drink the bottle). Drunk since sunrise, he would call in one or another offense unit. With an eloquence difficult to convey on paper, but which I had to hear regularly on the telephone (he could even recognize my voice), he would cry drunkenly, "It's you, Lotman (it was forbidden to call each other by our last names), well, you old so-and-so! Tell your people (and by this he meant the battalion commander, Pastushenko) that they sure as such-and-such better occupy the high point—such-and-such!—by the next call (that meant, by the next "cock crow")." Or, spraying saliva, in a drunken voice: "Pastushenko, Pastushenko, get the battalion up for attack, there ain't gonna be another Oder!" (This oft-repeated expression meant that we must not miss the opportunity to get the Hero of the Soviet Union or at least some other decent medal).

The battalion headquarters commander, an intelligent man and a good artilleryman, located in an area under thick enemy fire and full of mortars, would reply, "Yes sir," and lay down the receiver with fine profanity and the words, "Crawl there yourself." And later he would report that we had begun our attack, met with strong enemy fire, taken ground, and by evening he would announce, "We retreated to the starting line, losses are average."

The reader (if there will ever be a reader) might not understand the situation: the battalion commander understood that in losing his excellently trained soldiers for the sake of a drunken fool's medals, he was weakening the battery or the battalion. He was led by considerations neither of humanity nor indeed of anything else which people were not thinking of at the time, but rather by practical reason, which makes a man take care of his weapons, keep his subdivision prepared for combat, and feed his soldiers not out of pity but so they can work. All these shades of feeling are conveyed by means of Russian profanity, which expresses them beautifully and is perfectly understood by those listening.

But there were commanders who really threw their subdivisions into unnecessary and hopeless attacks, from sheer inexperience or vanity and thirst for decorations. We had long used the formula, "We retreated to the starting line," which was literal this time, and to this we came to add, "Twenty, thirty, etc., sticks fell," and thus we encrypted losses, losses of people, losses that were too great.

Some of the medal-lovers liked a phrase that some dashing journalist—I don't remember the newspaper—had used. The origin of the phrase was like this. In some official document was the sentence, "The artillery pursues the enemy with fire and wheels." As often happens, this rhetoric became a rule of conduct. The expression gained popularity. Of course, artillery does "pursue with fire and wheels," but each type of battery actually has its own form, without losing contact with the infantry. For instance, our guns might be in position for direct fire, and the firing might be at five kilometers. But for a flashy battle report, and in order to stun some touring journalist, and most importantly, to get decorations, it was advantageous for the commanders to represent it like this: *the artillerymen, gripped with enthusiasm, are longing for battle; the gun wheels can't be torn from the front line infantry units . . .*

The tank guns were forced to shoot at distances too close for them, rendering them virtually ineffective (for instance, in the time needed for heavy artillery to conduct one firing, a tank can accomplish ten of them). So a direct duel between heavy battery and advancing tanks usually has one outcome, which we repeatedly tested with personal experience: the battery manages to destroy one or two tanks, but at the cost of losing all its guns and personnel. Another consequence was that the artillery, enduring monstrous losses, would lose qualified and trained soldiers, be hastily replenished with younger ones, and as a result would no longer possess either the skill of quick and precise work or the most important element in the artillery: the coordination of the whole battery into a unified living being. The quality of the artillery would decline, and losses would increase, and yet with each breakthrough and movement forward the number of generals who had received hero medals and orders would increase.

Because of the great losses, the following occured: the army moved forward, as if gaining great, and in fact invaluable, experience—and therefore it had to increase the quality of its combat. But due to those enormous losses and the replenishment with totally inexperienced people, and also because the pursuit of medals turned into a real sickness by the end of the war, the quality of both combat and discipline in the unit decreased.

Looting, which was previously entirely unheard of, began during the offensive—and was often encouraged by headquarters officers, who had the means to carry the loot. At that time the use of the phrase "to organize" spread and became in vogue in our army—although we found it disgusting—to designate our looting, as the Germans did: for example, "I organized this radio for myself," or "to organize some new boots." When we entered Germany, this expression became trendy and came to refer to entering a house and taking this or that. I can say with full responsibility, however, that this never occured in our regiment.

Meanwhile, due to some of the more inventive string-pullers in the rear, looting was unofficially legitimized. As soon as we crossed the German border, we were told that we had the right to send packages home. Quantitative standards were introduced for privates and sergeants (I think the limit was six kilograms, but I don't remember for how long), but the higher-ranking officers quickly ceased to constrain themselves by any standards at all. I can admit that we seized a German train car carrying goods—I don't remember the station—and I sent home my alloted six kilograms of granulated sugar to post-blockade Leningrad. That was my only "trophy" (this word became the general term for appropriated things). My friends sent home sugar or other goods seized from storehouses, that is, whatever they could rightfully call a war trophy.

Not only did we refuse to participate in the widespread looting, we also openly expressed our disgust for it. On the other hand, we had a different method: after a firing there would be empty copper cartridge cases left on the battery (for our shells, the cases were metallic tubings, bigger than half a man), and they had to be sent back to the rear. Our boys would stuff them full of trophy foodstuffs or junk from stores, and I would repeatedly hear, "Why not let our women be happy for a while, since they're running around practically naked now." But under all the extenuating circumstances, the opportunity to loot, whatever you call it, corrupted the army. Later, when the front line army turned into an occupying force, looting didn't diminish, but rather increased. Front line soldiers were demobilized, and the units were replenished with entirely young village guys, and these guys went totally beserk at the opportunities opened up for them by the uncontrolled position of the status of the occupying soldier, since they were so accustomed to hunger and destitution.

But corruption starts at the top. Whatever a soldier could loot (and by now it wasn't only appropriated bags of sugar from the German army reserves, but the property of civilians) was still totally incomparable with the opportunities of the generals, who took broad advantage of those opportunities. It is not a justification when I say that the American army, with whom we later had a lot of contact, looted no less than we did, only with greater understanding and discrimination. For us it was all a wonder; *they* knew to select real value.

Two days before the war ended officially, our regiment (which at first was converted to a guard regiment, and then repeatedly awarded various combat medals and became a brigade, having preserved our own spirit and the backbone of our commanders nearly 'til the end of the war) ended up on the Oder, when we ran into the Americans. We split up onto both banks of the river. An SS unit was stranded on a long island in the middle of the river, where it preferred to surrender to the Americans, and warded off our attacks until the very last minute.

Evening came, and we suddenly, unexpectedly realized that the war was over. It was strange—I can't think of a more precise word. It's probably how an infant feels when he's just been born: the familiar situation is gone, and he doesn't know what to do.

We didn't manage to drink with the Americans right then—that happened a few days later. We got some very weak, sour, homemade apple wine from somewhere and drank it in the dark, on the shore, which was already entirely devoid of both people and danger. And there something strange happened.

The general mood of those years, as I've said, was cheerful. There was sometimes fatigue, and curses, and occasionally our energy and strength were only sustained by means of lengthy and sophisticated profanities (which is very effective). In general, it was no idyll. But it was totally different in comparison with what happened to us immediately upon the end of the war. For some reason we became incredibly sad.

In a number of films that represent the end of the war, there are always shots of solemn reunions between these front line soldiers and their girlfriends and families who have endured every hardship. But months passed between the end of the war and even the first insignificant demobilization. Those were the hardest months.

We were in a kind of sparse grove. We weren't burdened with

chores (the usual torment of a soldier in non-combat conditions); we were free. If we wanted to, we could even go to a nearby German village or a very nice neighboring little town. But suddenly, and seemingly without reason, we were gripped by oppressively dull anguish—not boredom, but precisely this dull anguish. We drank like dead men and never got drunk. I had to remember and realize all that I had been studiously forgetting during those years.

There was a somewhat boring older man in the next regiment over, one of the reservists, who was fulfilling his role as a small-time political worker, which we didn't respect at all. He was a little drunk. He came to sit down with me and, crying (although until this moment there had been no intimacy between us at all) and wiping his snot with his elbow, began to talk, addressing me informally. He began to recount that his village had been burned, that his kids were with their aunt, and that he still had no idea where his wife was. And I myself also had something to recall, although I didn't tell him (it was hidden away too deeply).

It had happened in the Orkhonka station, in Kuban. It was in 1942, when the southern front drove directly up to Ordzhonikidze, which wasn't called Vladikavkaz yet, and our regiment was directly covering the way to the city. If we didn't manage to detain the tank convoys here, then Ordzhonikidze would fall by lunchtime. The day before, we were removed from Mozdok. We opened a communication line, and the battery only had time to dig a few trenches when, with the first morning light, a hurricane of fire began from the German side.

For me personally, events unfolded in a natural way: our communication line was broken. I ran along the line (the accursed fate of a telephonist—when everything gets jammed up in the trenches, he runs along the line and connects broken wires). Our wire was conveyed across the Orkhonka—a tributary of the Terek, where local women often came to get water. When I ran up to the Orkhonka, I saw something that has stayed with me my whole life: a woman, naturally not knowing that our front lines had come in the night, and that the night before we had been thirteen kilometers away, if not more— this woman had come right up and out onto the street, and come to the river for water, having brought with her a little three- or four-year-old boy. An exploded shell had struck her in the temple, and she was lying—I can see it now—with spread legs, her skirt thrown back, with a little runny red stain on her temple. And next to her the little boy, who didn't understand what had happened, was pulling her by the hand. Did I do the right thing? This question haunts me still. I think about it constantly and I often picture this scene. I had a broken line, and that meant that the battery was paralyzed. By the intensity of the German fire it was clear that in a few minutes a mass tank attack would begin, and the battery would be silent. I had to connect the wires, and I ran further along the line. In that moment I had no doubts about what I should do.

The line was already broken several times by shrapnel, and I ran from this side to that, connecting test phones, eliminating the new damage. When the artillery fire ceased and the German tanks rolled back without breaking through, I headed along the line back to my position, having totally forgotten about that incident. Suddenly, near our wire, in the same place where I had connected it, I saw a puddle of blood (later, some women told me that they had dragged the child home; the mother, of course, had been killed on the spot). I must admit that it did not make a particular impression on me at the time. As Speransky said to Baten'kov: "When you live in a cemetery, you can't mourn them all." But on the first drunken night after the end of the war I saw it all over again. This moment and many others. It was not an accident that we would get dead drunk and that there were even several suicides. These were later officially written off as "under the influence of alcohol," as they later defined Fadeev's suicide, but the real cause, of course, was different. The time to pay off our debts had come. Just as it later came for Fadeev. (I'll note in parentheses that it's impossible for me not to respect Fadeev for being an honest debtor. I'm not.)

We became so sick of staying in the army that it was unbearable, and demobilization was still in some far-distant future. Our commanders, wishing to maintain discipline, assured us that we would not be demobilized at all, but deployed to China. We drank the cup of death.

A solution unexpectedly turned up. There was a lieutenant, Tolya Tomashevich, in our regiment. He was the son of a lady who was well-known in Moscow's intelligentsia circles, and who in her second marriage was married to one of the most senior generals, a professor in the Artillery Academy, a nobleman who had switched over to the Red Army as far back as the Civil War. Now he was half in disfavor: he was a respected officer, but he'd been taken out of the direct line of command. His stepson Tolya had ended up in a camp through entirely trivial antics (when he was a student before the war, he started a handwritten literary magazine called "Hoo-ryay!"). When the war began, the stepfather-general, the mentor of a number of young marshalls, managed to get his stepson out of the camp and sent to the front. Smart, brave, and extremely artistically talented, Tolya quickly rose to the rank of lieutenant on the front and picked up some medals, and when the war ended, he decided to organize a front line theater. With the support of some generals, he received permission and gathered a group of maybe fifty of our very talented boys around him. The army is like Noah's ark. You can find two of anything in it. An excellent violinist was found, and several professional accordionists, and a remarkable juggler. His signature act was walking on a tightrope, carrying a heavy table on his nose. His tightrope was stretched so as to cross the front row where the generals and headquarters staff sat, and the cool thing was that he was always about to drop the heavy table with the two side tables, but would ultimately return it to its original position. One time, he had brilliantly performed his number, and when he finally set the table down and bowed, the brigade commander burst into a rage and shouted, "Five days under arrest!"

In this homemade theater I took an artist's role: I drew the stage sets. When we did scenes from ancient theater, we put up a bunch of sets that I had designed, all depicting ancient goddesses. The chief of the political department thought that we had dragged it all out from the German theater reserves in the basement, and said, "This German whore—take her down immediately." And when I reported that it wasn't German, that I had drawn it yesterday, his jaw dropped and he said, "You drew that? You're kidding me!"

So we created a hotbed of art in a rather unusual situation. We also had some glitches. Tolya artfully imitated a stammer, and this was his trademark act. One day he didn't take into account that the audience in the hospital where we were performing were all shell-shocked, and that many of them stammered. After his act, which he carried through brilliantly, he nearly got beaten up and had to hide.

Despite all this "merriment," things were really hard emotionally: we were all longing to get home, and we were realizing at the same time that we were estranged from the life that was waiting for us. We had no profession and we were going into the unknown.

In many situations, unfortunately, our fears came true. Among us was a guy from Rostov—a born actor, with great tragic facial expressiveness and God-given theatrical gestures. While he was still in the army he had taken to drinking ether, and soon after the demobilization, we received notice that he had died.

Finally it was time to demobilize.

On the way home I ran into the son of the woman who cleaned our street. He had been taken prisoner, but fortunately, when the front collapsed, he had been drafted into the army from captivity (this happened very rarely; prisoners of war were usually sent straight to the camps) and demobilized as a soldier. We arrived in Leningrad late at night; the train car pulled over somewhere onto the emergency tracks; no one came to meet us. I hadn't written home to tell the exact date, because it was impossible to specify return dates, and I didn't want to worry them for no reason. We stopped the first vehicle we saw—it was an ambulance. We had some money and the driver agreed to drive us all home for a small sum, after he dropped off his patient. So I arrived home in the middle of the night. Everyone was asleep at home—they hadn't been expecting me. The next day I went to the university.

I re-enrolled at the university and went to work with the thirst of an alcoholic. I would run from the university to the Public Library and stay there right until it closed. It was an entirely palpable sense of happiness. I had to decide on a seminar. G. A. Gukovsky was the general idol of the students. I demonstrated my independence and did not choose Gukovsky but registered instead to work with N. I.

Mordovchenko, who was still considered a young professor, and not as popular. But under Mordovchenko, who worked on Belinsky, I selected a topic on Karamzin—that is, one of Gukovsky's topics. I didn't think it would bother anyone. But Gukovsky was apparently offended.

I have never in my life experienced anything more exciting than my work in those days on the article "Karamzin in *The Herald of Europe*." I really regret that the work was not fully published and that a significant portion of it was later lost. Karamzin declared that *The Herald of Europe* would be a journal fully devoted to translations and would publish information on the latest events in Europe. He indicated his sources very opaquely or did not indicate them at all. My work was looking for sources. It was a totally incomparable delight to sit in an empty room in the Public Library where all the French journals were, and to dig into them until I'd get kicked out. It soon became evident that Karamzin very inaccurately indicated his sources and in fact had been publishing not translations but very tendentious retellings, which had been done with a distinct orientation towards the events of Russian life. For instance, I was able to prove that Karamzin had personally responded to the death of Radishchev, having disguised his response under a translation from the French.

This still-unpublished article is my very favorite to this day.

I spent whole days in the stacks of the Public Library. And meanwhile, things were moving quickly and very threateningly. A campaign against cosmopolitanism was launched. Somehow it crept up on me unnoticed. First were the attacks on Eikhenbaum. But somehow the seriousness of these attacks didn't reach my consciousness. Especially because there had recently been a university anniversary during which Eikhenbaum had received a state decoration. After the first articles in the papers, which I took to be nonsense, not worth taking seriously, I repeated these words from *Macbeth* to myself: "The earth hath bubbles, as the water has, / And these are of them." And it seemed to me that it had nothing to do with me personally, and that these "bubbles" would vanish just as they arrived.

Once, when I was heading over to Mordovchenko's (every visit was an event for me, and I would nervously stand for a long time on the stairwell before I rang the bell), I found him frightened and worried. Lowering his voice, although this conversation took place inside his apartment, he told me that in Moscow the Jewish Anti-fascist Committee had been arrested. I completely didn't understand why he was so shaken; all kinds of people got arrested in those days. Later, events began to unfold very quickly in accordance with a pre-arranged program.

And all this time I was still running over to the Public Library and to the archives. When events directly entered university walls and these devastating "assessments" and purges of Eikhenbaum, Gukovsky, Zhirmunsky, and other professors began to occur, I couldn't understand for a long time what the matter was (during this campaign, a proofreader named Babkin was sent from the Pushkin House to the university for "reinforcement," and he became a professor).

K. Azadovsky has very effectively collected and presented the details of the devastation of the university and of the Pushkin House and published his work in collaboration with B. F. Egorov. So I'll only treat what concerned me personally.

The time came for job placement. It worked like this: the commission would meet in the main building at night (they usually began work after eleven). Before this, we would stand in the hallway and wait. Then the door would open (the ritual was to keep the conference hall dense with smoke, so that when the door opened, smoke would pour out like from hell). And sitting there were Berdnikov, Fedya Abramov (until then he had been a party functionary and leading thug and later he became a famous writer[11]), and the rest of the party bureau.

I was called; I went in; they looked at me, even though they knew me and I knew them inside and out; and they said, "Step outside, wait a little while, it's still too early" (I did not understand why they called me in). This rite resembled the one thought up by Nicholas

---

11 Just before his Candidate's exams, he called me for advice on Radishchev. It really struck me that he kept smoking the whole time, and sticking his cigarette butts to the wall with spit, and repeating, "Okay, I just need the basics, no extra stuff."

I, when the condemned Poles were run through the gauntlet in a certain order, so that the head of the uprising went through last and he had to watch all his companions beaten to death. Our procedure was less solemn, but it still had its "knolls and brooks." Leningrad girls from nice families, "drawing-room" families, were sent without any official objection to Siberian villages or to the Far East. I had to watch all this while waiting my turn. Finally they called me, looked at me, and for some reason spoke to me in the third person: "Let him come back another time." Finally, I was called back to Berdnikov in a few days and he announced that I'd been given the opportunity to look for a job on my own. When I asked Berdnikov where the references that I'd been given in the brigade during demobilization were,[12] he looked me in the eye with his own clear eyes and said distinctly, "They're lost." That was the price I'd paid to be allowed to find job placement on my own.

Then the long period of looking for work began. It progressed according to a fully stereotypical scenario. Mornings I would set out to one of the places where I'd seen a job opening the night before (usually a school). The director would receive me very kindly, would say that they did indeed have a vacancy, and ask me to come in the next day with my application and to fill out the job questionnaires. Strangely enough, in 1950 I still had that quality which, depending on your point of view, you might call either naïveté or stupidity. My entire experience had thus far been related to war, so for me, the meaning of filling out the questionnaires was entirely unclear. When I first ran into my acquaintance, a cheerful cynic named Dimka Moldavsky (before the war, he and I had been in the same class, but he suffered from a heart condition and never went to the front; by this time he was already a graduate student working on Mayakovsky under Naumov), he asked me, "Who did you come back as?" I didn't understand the question. "Like, what's your fifth paragraph, idiot?"

---

12 The references had been written by a battalion clerk, who had been a soldier in my platoon. We had gotten along well. The battalion commander had signed it, but of course all the laudatory epithets had come from the clerk writer: it turned out that I had nearly single-handedly defeated the beast of Fascism in its very own lair.

(Dimka's mother was Russian, and he was a Russian according to his passport.) After he explained I strongly protested and told him to get lost. The very formulation of the question seemed insane to me.

My education on this matter was completed by A. V. Zapadov—an intelligent man, given to mockery and cynicism. Once I ran into him in the Philology Department and complained to him that it seemed like there were job openings, except for the repetition of this one and the same strange procedure: first, a detailed and very promising interview, then a request that I fill out a questionnaire, a suggestion that I come back in a couple of days, and after that, some kind of strange glance to the side and always the same formula: "You know, unfortunately, this opening was taken away from us yesterday." Zapadov looked at me like I was an idiot. I hadn't seen such a dumbfounded face in a long time. "You don't know what the matter is?" he asked me. "No, I don't know." "You know what, get over to the zoological museum, they need someone with a philological education, go talk to them." I set off. When I dropped in at the office of the deputy director, a fat older Jew, I told him that Zapadov had sent me. The guy looked at me with undisguised indignation. "What'd he send you for? I've explained to him that we've already got two Jews working here. I can't take any more." I turned and left. In a couple of days I ran into Zapadov on the street. "You get it now?" he asked. "Got it," I said. "All right then," he said, "you can't get rich on dreams."

However, the reserve of postwar optimism (or perhaps stupidity?) was so great that my mood was at that moment feisty and merry. I continued to write my dissertation (I wrote a long article on Pnin, which wasn't published anywhere, although I thought the article made sense).

I also began a rather vague relationship with Zara Grigorievna. We'd met when I was in my fourth year at university. During this time I was earning some money on the side drawing square-by-square portraits of leaders. What came out only faintly resembled the originals (especially at the beginning). But that didn't matter. My clients were usually majors or colonels who had run military clubs, and they looked on only to ensure that all the medals were carefully depicted, and once they were sure that everything was alright in that department, they would decide that the portraits could be hung.

Incidentally, I learned the art of painting square-by-square por-traits while working in our army club. In order for you to imagine what constitutes resemblance from a military point of view, I'll re-count the following episode. After the end of the war, our brigade stayed in Potsdam. Wishing to avoid the insufferably boring march drills and excercises in the deployment of firing positions, which were completely senseless after the war, I started working, as I've already said, as an artist at the club. My partner was my close friend Khachik Galiumsrian—a really talented artist and very sweet guy. Together we learned the art of drawing square-by-square portraits.

One day we were informed that there would be a meeting at the club, at which a candidate for the Supreme Soviet, from the group of occupying forces, would speak—a man named Abakumov. This name, which at that time frightened even the bravest of people, meant nothing to me. In Tynianov's novella, there is a sentence ex-plaining why the condemnned lieutenant isn't brought to the gal-lows and some empty boxes are stood in his place: "The criminal is secret; he has no body." Abakumov was, in part, a secret boss. There was some kind of totally incomprehensible clouded blot on the posters with portraits and biographies of the candidates (which were mandatory, according to ritual). Even the medals were impos-sible to make out, but they were listed in the printed biography. We broke this blot into little squares and drew something absolutely im-possible. Thanks to the simplicity of the mores of the time, we were allowed to enter the club where Abakumov was to speak before the voters and were easily admitted to our usual places (the hall lighting was also my responsibility). When Abakumov took the floor, Kha-chik and I looked at each other and nearly fell over. In front of us was nothing even remotely similar to our blot. But we were reckless then and we weren't scared. We just laughed. With his light Arme-nian accent, which he would strengthen during particularly comic moments, Khachik said to me, "Don't worry about it, I'll just go up to him and say, 'Comrade Abakumov, look, let me break your snout into little squares,' and we'll sketch him fast."

One day after lecture, Zara Grigorievna and Vika Kamenskaya

came up to me, and Zara Grigorievna asked me to decorate the hall for the next scholarly conference, which was devoted to Mayakovsky—and in particular, to draw his portrait. I was saving all my time for my studies, to which I had given myself with the same passion that draws the alcoholic to the bottle. Participating in such activities wasn't part of my plans. Stuttering badly (when I was an artilleryman, working on the telephone, I worked out the right breathing and almost never stuttered, but after demobilization, in the "civilian world," I suddenly discovered that I stuttered worse than ever during conversations with girls or with strangers; once at a group meeting I had to cancel my presentation and left the stage), I explained to Zara Grigorievna that I only painted for money. Such cynicism shook her Komsomol enthusiasm, and she stepped away from me with tears in her eyes, uttering loudly, "Scum with a mustache!" That was our first conversation.

Our next encounter was even less successful. At the student scholarly conference devoted to Belinsky, Zara Grigorievna, with the cavalier audacity typical of her at the time, decided to give a presentation on "Belinsky and Romanticism." It was not a good presentation. It basically failed. Mark Kachurin, with his usual insight, gently pointed out that the presenter had not derived the very concept of Romanticism from historical sources but from widespread clichés. In just as principled a way, and as tactfully as ever, P. I. Mordovchenko also spoke. The devil moved me to speak as an advocate for the defense, and so, stuttering badly, I uttered some liberal sentences about how on the one hand, of course, well, but on the other hand, it was impossible not to appreciate that . . . The presenter stoically endured all the criticism. But she could not endure my defense of her and ran to the ladies' room, and all the girls trailed after her in a solemn procession. Of course, tact required that I simply withdraw. But I decided that my duty as a man was to provide comfort—that is, the worst thing that I could imagine. I waited until Zara Grigorievna and the other ladies abandoned their sanctuary and then foisted myself onto them so as to escort them home. (We later remembered this episode as a criterion of complete idiocy; it became one of our family legends.)

In the future, our relations improved, and the night before her state examination, I was invited as a consultant who would "pump" Zara, Vika, and Lyuda Lakaeva full of information on the 18th and 19th centuries (they were great fans of D. E. Maksimov, and they studied Blok, all of Blok, and nothing but Blok).

Before my trip to Tartu, I had walked not only over the enormous territory of the Soviet Union, but had also crossed Poland, Germany, and the Baltic states on foot. However, the soldier's feeling of being abroad is totally different from the civilian's. As Lev Tolstoy has said, a soldier, even if he crosses the whole world, is still always located in the same regiment space: the same sergeant major, the same battalion dog, the same responsibilities and interests. Even in various entanglements, in numerous retreats and encirclements, when the soldier was sometimes left by himself and had to track his regiment alone for a hundred kilometers—the image of the regiment was constantly present. It was like a glass through which the rest of the world could be seen: a direction, the objectives, the nature of action—everything was predetermined. And if you had to manifest the greater concentration of your individual will, then that will was directed at your being able to merge with that space again.

Now there was a fundamentally different set of circumstances. Each of us had to decide his own fate. We had gone into the army as boys and returned as grown men. We had learned responsibility. Under specific formulaic circumstances, we had unmistakably known what we had to do to be honorable people. But now we found ourselves in entirely different circumstances—for which we didn't have any kind of clichéd formulae. We were used to being adults, making important decisions, and at the same time we were having the experience of being children, being totally unprepared for regular situations. And circumstances threw us into the political situation of the second half of the 1940s, which categorically demanded a choice of conduct and individual responsibility. One peculiarity was that when the icedrift of time split up and spread its ice blocks around, it often happened that people who still hadn't forgotten their recent wartime ties turned up on very different floating blocks of ice.

Something similar affected my relationship with Georgy Petrovich

Berdnikov. Berdnikov, a classmate of my sister Lida, along with Ma-kogonenko and Kukulevich, was nearly destitute during his student years. He would certainly not have held onto his seat as a student if not for Gukovsky. Gukovsky noticed this capable student, who was oppressed by destitution and political hardships, and by the laws that bound the old professoriate, made every effort to help him. He provided Berdnikov with financial assistance, and helped him turn a term paper into an article and publish it in the student volume of the department's "Scholarly Proceedings".

On the eve of the 1940 New Year, Lida's class gathered, in accordance with tradition, in our huge apartment, and I hung around with the students. I remember that when the clock struck midnight, Berdnikov lifted his glass[13] in his hands and uttered: "Guys! We're the men of the '40s! Let's drink to the '40s!" And everyone drank together. And indeed the '40s began.

After the war, at university, I ran into Berdnikov again. I was in my second year; he was a graduate student. We were both wearing military shirts, but there were captain's stars on his epaulets. In the war he had served in the headquarters of the infantry regiment, and I think he was a good soldier. This, his frequenting our apartment, and his marriage to Tanya Vanovskaya—a charming, lovely girl, a friend and classmate of Lida's (to whom I was not indifferent, as I remember)—all this had already added a shade of nuance to our relationship even before he began his dizzying career path. While trying to maintain objectivity, I can say that Berdnikov was not unintelligent, was cruel only to the extent that was necessary in his career (in which case he was merciless), destroyed people according to cold calculation but without pleasure—and you know, that means a lot. At the first opportunity he tried to wash his hands of these doings, at least a little. So, for instance, after becoming Director of the Theater Institute (having neither any relation to theater nor to the scholarly direction of the Institute, but having the kind of status that meant he could be the Director of who cares what), he tried to go back to working with some of the people who had been driven out in the

13 They were our family's old glasses, but I can't imagine what we drank out of them—I only remember that of course we had no champagne.

era of anti-cosmopolitanism, people like Yakov Bilinkis, and Berd-nikov even gained a reptuation as a progressive in Leningrad theater and humanities circles. In fact he was an intelligent, absolutely un-principled person, who clearly understood that the whole ideological witches' sabbath wouldn't last long and that those who use the bones of others to climb so quickly to the top will just as quickly collapse to the bottom. His intuition didn't deceive him. He wanted a different fate for himself and he fashioned it, and after he made a few sharp turns, he comfortably lived his whole life through.

Two options lay before me: keep looking for work in Leningrad, knocking on these doors that were closed to me, or else spit, throw down my cards, and start some kind of totally different game. And I chose the second. There was a sweet girl from Leningrad named Olya Zaichikova who was in my year at school. Our relationship consisted in our sometimes chatting if we ran into each other in the library or the Philology Dept. hallways. Her fiancé had been killed in the war; our relations were warm, but rather distant. Once when Olya and I met up, we talked about what was going on with each of us, and she found out that I was unsuccessfully looking for work, that I was totally fed up with it, and that I wanted to spit on it all and get the hell out of Leningrad (at that time I imagined that a village school lay before me, and I was already gathering together my books to take away with me). She suggested that I make a phone call to Tartu, to the Teachers' Institute where she was appointed, and where she knew there was an opening in Russian Literature. I called Institute Director Tarnik. He listened to all my statistics and said that I could come.

Dressed in a slightly taken-in black suit of my father's, which was my only "holiday" suit, I went to Tartu, and I stayed there for the rest of my life.

Ignorance of the language and of the state of affairs—in addi-tion to the unconscionable foolishness that has accompanied me throughout my entire life—prevented me from seeing the tragedy of the circumstances in which we found ourselves. I sincerely per-ceived the situation as an idyll: working with students gave me great pleasure; an excellent library allowed me to energetically push along the chapters of my dissertation, which was largely already written;

friendship with a group of young literary scholars who lived in Tartu—all this gave me a feeling of continuous happiness. Four to six hours of lecturing per day didn't wear me out, and the unexpected discovery that in the course of giving lectures I was able to arrive at fundamentally new ideas, and that interesting concepts, previously unknown to me, would emerge by the end of class, gave me wings.

My dissertation was virtually written while I was still a student, and I submitted it for defense immediately after I graduated university (I think this was interpreted as impudence, but it was honestly just naïveté).

My official discussants were P. N. Berkov and A. V. Predtechensky. At the time of my Candidate's defense my doctorate was practically already finished. Important events were happening at this point in my life. I got a new job at the university (the number of students grew, and an additional vacancy appeared; Rector F. Klement recommended me for it). And I got married. Zara Grigorievna moved to Tartu (I had to overcome her desperate resistance: she didn't want to leave her school, and as I told her maliciously, she was going to "build socialism in one classroom").

The formalizing of our relationship was very much in the spirit of Zara Grigorievna's Komsomol maximalism. We set off to the registration bureau to "tie the knot." Neither Zara Grigorievna nor I expected to take off our coats when we got there. But I still wore my "lecturing" suit (in our family's language this was my "smoke and gloom"—the left sleeve was smudged with stearin oil, because the lights went out at night and I had to work by candlelight). Zara Grigorievna didn't have any kind of nice dress (petty bourgeois!). But she found a "surrogate," something sewn from her Aunt Manya's dress—a woman quite twice the size and girth of Zara Grigorievna.

We arrived at the registry office. "Arrived" isn't quite the word: I literally dragged the desperately resisting Zara Grigorievna, who was saying that first of all, she would not move to Tartu and leave behind her Volkhov students, and second of all, domestic life was totally petty bourgeois (Zara Grigorievna's friend Lyuda summarized all this talk with the caustic formula, "The personal affairs belong to the behind; the public goals should be put forward!") In the registry office an exceptionally nice Estonian man was waiting for us. He had kept his post under all the regime changes, and, like most intellectuals of his age at that time, he spoke Russian very well. First of all, he dealt us a decisive blow in offering to take our coats. Zara Grigorievna was suddenly struck with a fit of laughter (and not at all hysterical; she really found the whole "petty bourgeois" procedure funny). The head of the registry office looked at us mournfully and uttered with profound understanding, "Yes, the first time it really is funny!" After that we had a wedding feast. We invited Shanygin, a lecturer at the university. (I spent a few months in his room before I received my own small separate room.)[14] The feast consisted of two cups of coffee each and a whole tray of pastries with whipped cream, *vastlakuklid.*

I was assigned a room in a "consolidated" apartment where the director of a grocery store lived—an exceptionally nice man. He was Estonian, had married a Latvian woman, and spoke Russian at home. His wife was a real lady; she never worked and led quite a worldly life. She kept the apartment in ideal order and dusted every day with a white cloth. Our room, which was littered with books and never exactly shone from tidiness, aroused squeamish disgust in her. But it became worse when our son was born, and Nanny Stepanida[15] came to stay with us from Pskov and quickly disseminated these huge terrible cockroaches, the likes of which I had never seen in my life and certainly never saw again.

The kitchen doors closed right in front of us, and we had to cook for four people, including an infant, on a kerosene stove in the hallway. Stepanida would invariably fall asleep at the stove after having demolished all available edible reserves, and the kerosene

---

14 Shanygin was a bachelor by conviction. We never cleaned up—the floor was ankle-deep in trash. He would call up ladies he knew and always deliver the same text: "Yulenka! (or Tanechka, Sashenka, etc.) I haven't slept for three nights (he was distinctive in his enviably deep sleep and terrible snoring). I bared my soul before myself and realized—oh, no, I don't deserve you at all. You're pure, you're— holy!" After that, a readiness either to fall from the heights of purity or to raise him to them would begin to sound through the telephone receiver, but he would continue: "You do not know the full extent of my depravity. Farewell—forever."

15 This is an anachronism: Stepanida was much later. I don't remember this nanny's name. (Mikhail Lotman's note)

stove would begin to smoke. When we arrived home from our lectures, it was impossible to get in. Misha was blackened like an African child, Stepanida was asleep[16], and the neighbor had passed out.

But we lived very merrily: we worked a lot, we wrote a lot, and we spent a lot of time with a small but quite close and quite friendly crowd. I began to work at the university full time, and Zara Grigorievna worked at the Teachers' Institute.

Around this time, B. F. Egorov came to Tartu. Rector Klement had invited his wife Sonya, a chemist, to work in Tartu. Boris Fedorovich was in his fifth year at the Institute of Aviation Engineering, but he was nearly finished. This promised him a secure future, which was no trifle at that time. He had the courage to sharply change the direction of his life, finish at Leningrad State University in the Folklore Department by correspondence, come to Tartu as a graduate student in folkore at the Herzen Institute, and—having quickly defended his dissertation—become a member of the Literature Department. When B. V. Pravdin retired, Egorov became the chair. He transferred his friend, the young and exceptionally talented Yakov Bilinkis, to Tartu to take the vacancy that appeared after Adams was arrested.

In Tartu there was a small but hardworking group of people who were constantly having discussions and exchanging ideas on various theoretical and historico-literary topics. We would often get together and argue for hours. The discussions between Bilinkis and myself were especially pointed. I had been raised on formalism since my student years, and was thus attracted to structural ideas. Boris Fedorovich was also drawn to them. But Bilinkis had a sharp negative reaction to structuralism: he called it the "dehumanization of the humanities" and defended intuitionism as a matter of principle. An exceptionally talented lecturer, he would have liked to introduce subjective improvisation to the literary sciences.

All in all, we lived in an intense and very attractive atmosphere. Whenever we escaped to Leningrad or to Moscow, it was only to dig ourselves up to the ears in archives.

---

16 According to my parents, the nanny would always wake up and race to the kerosene stove with the same formula: "Damnit—we're smoked out!" (Mikhail Lotman's note)

V.

In old Tartu style, the doors of the house that we (that is, Zara Grigorievna, the children, and I) lived in never locked. In Tartu this was unexceptional. Entering from the street through a tiny little hallway, you could go straight through our largest room, which was our dining room, our living room, and my office at the same time.

One Sunday morning, when Zara Grigorievna, the children, and I were sitting down to breakfast, someone came in energetically from the stairs and pounded on the door. In the doorway stood a tall man. Both his face and stance expressed that he was ready to start a fight.

In general, we were besieged by correspondence students. After they failed their exams, often they wouldn't go away, because they would only receive their travel allowance upon successfully completing their coursework. I decided that this was another failed student who would now attempt to prove that he fully deserved a C. But the situation turned out to be different.

The newcomer introduced himself. It turned out to be Solzhenitsyn, who had just thundered out his first short novel, *One Day in the Life of Ivan Denisovich.* I don't remember how he introduced himself, but it followed from his words and gestures that he had come to punch me in the face. In order to explain, let's go back a little in time. At this point our senior classes were pretty strong. It became increasingly possible to introduce innovations to the program, and Zara Grigorievna took enthusiastic advantage of these possibilities. The course on Soviet Literature quickly became interesting. We managed to squeeze the "Laureates" a bit and stick in some émigré literature and some repressed writers at their expense. This was all entirely new. There was nothing like it either in Leningrad or in Moscow.

So a small group of students formed in the department who were actively studying the works of Bulgakov under Zara Grigorievna. One promising student who took part in these activities was a very capable young man from a local Russian community, but he had been an alcoholic and a kleptomaniac since childhood (which we didn't know). On the recommendation of Zara Grigorievna and myself, he was hospitably received by Elena Sergeevna Bulgakova, and allowed to read a typewritten copy of the not-yet published novel *Master and Margarita*. After a while he began showing up in our department with a manuscript of the novel (it wasn't the first copy, but it did have some of the author's corrections penciled in). He assured us that he'd gotten the manuscript legally from Elena Sergeevna.

Hence unfolded a totally Bulgakovian story. Elena Sergeevna anxiously reported to us that the draft of *Master and Margarita* had been stolen and that she was extremely worried because of negotiations with Simonov about the publication (the negotiations were rather hopeless and protracted, but they were still going on) and if the manuscript slipped away and was published abroad, then the possibility of publishing it in the USSR would be closed forever (at that time, it seemed like forever). I went to the house of the student in question—he lived on the very edge of Tartu in a solid, totally merchant-style house, probably built in the 1910s, with an abundant fruit orchard and a tall gate that locked. Inside, my eyes immediately fell on a number of my books that had gone missing. I acted somewhat theatrically, in the spirit of Marquis de Posa—which is shameful to recount now, but you can't leave lyrics out of a song. I made a theatrical gesture and in the voice of Schiller's hero I uttered, "You have need of these books? I bestow them unto you!" (Of course, I should have behaved more simply, but that was how I did it, and this theatricality did apparently have some kind of effect.) After that I whirled around and said, I think again in the voice of Marquis de Posa, something to the effect that if any honor at all remained in his heart, he should bring me Bulgakov's manuscript before dusk, and that I wasn't about to rummage around in his things and do a proper search. After that I left.

I waited for the thief at home but he didn't show up. At night (Zara Grigorievna and the children were already asleep), I sat with my desk lamp in the dark room and waited. Sometime around two in the morning, footsteps resounded on the stairs. Through the slightly open door a hand slipped in and dropped a letter onto the hall table (this letter should be in my archive). After that the steps retreated and the door slammed shut.

The letter was absolutely horrible. Only a mixture of Svidrigailov and Marmeladov could write such a letter. It was repentant, with disgusting particulars and a touch of the holy fool—entirely in the spirit of Dostoevsky. The letter reported that the manuscript was returned to Elena Sergeevna (detail: the packet was sent by unregistered post, even though the difference in cost was just a few miserable kopecks, and unregistered mail often got lost).

This episode effectively closed off the possibility of a place in a graduate program for our hero, which would have doubtless belonged to him. In accordance with his job placement, he went off to a suburban school near his home, where he soon drank himself to death. Incidentally, he had been a very handsome guy.

But this story has an unexpected sequel. I already knew from Elena Sergeevna that the incident was settled (she was offended that it had been sent by regular mail, and since I was the involuntary accomplice to this whole dirty story, I felt bad whenever I saw her after that, although I never heard any recriminations or accusations from her side). But it turned out that Elena Sergeevna didn't know for some time that the manuscript had been sent to her. And it was during this "some time" that I heard that energetic knock on the door one Sunday morning. Fortunately, I was able to calm Solzhenitsyn down in the very first words that I spoke, with the news that the manuscript had already been sent to Elena Sergeevna and that if it hadn't already arrived, it should get there today or tomorrow.

Our conversation immediately took a different direction. I don't remember what we talked about, but at the center of it was *One Day in the Life of Ivan Denisovich*, and the issue of arranging the brilliant astronomer N. N. to come to the Estonian Observatory or the Physics Institute—he had been released from the camps, and wanted to empirically test the theoretical calculations regarding the allocations of the elements of air (or some kind of gas?) on the moon, and the possibility of some form of simple life—the astronomer was out of work. We parted entirely peacefully, and on that same day I went to go see him in his hotel and we walked around Tartu for rather a long time. Later we wrote each other a few letters. Unfortunately, we never met up again.

VI.

In the late '60s, Natalya Gorbanevskaya often visited Tartu with her son (he was the same age as Lyosha). We already knew her, and I really liked her poetry, and our two families got very close. She lived with us at our dacha in the summer and in Tartu with my niece Natasha. It was her style to carry herself with pointed fearlessness. At that apartment, she conducted meetings of a conspiratorial nature, although we couldn't really call it conspiracy—she despised that at the root. We were already being watched carefully, and she knew that and deliberately defied it.

As a result, we had a very turbulent and merry summer. In the fall, Gorbanevskaya brought me a whole packet of papers for safekeeping. I had a tall chiminey in my office and I put everything on top of it. Sinner that I am, to this day I still don't know what was in that packet, as I don't like to rifle through other people's papers. I don't remember how many weeks passed (Gorbanevskaya had left for Moscow), when, early in the morning, someone rang and I opened the door. Without introducing themselves, without asking permission, about twelve men entered.[17] I knew some of them. One was the husband of one of my students, a notorious drunk—later he came by specially to apologize to me and express how ashamed he was for taking part in the search. At the time he smelled of vodka, which, as we all know, arouses the conscience.[18] But apparently it wasn't just

---

17 The number of participants in the search and their rudeness are both somewhat exaggerated. Although I wasn't in Tartu at the time, I can judge by fresher retellings of this story. The formula with which they entered became a family catchphrase: "Happy New Year, Yuri Mikhailovich, I wish you happiness. You probably don't remember me: I'm K., a prosecution employee. Look, we've come with a search warrant." This all took place in early January of 1970. (Mikhail Lotman's note)

18 It's a common folk characteristic: a guy may be a villain, but when he gets drunk, he comes to atone. So it was with S.—he'd get drunk and come over: "Yurka, I'm a villain, I'm a creep, I'm a snitch. But I never snitched on you" (he only addressed me this informally when he was drunk). When the KGB couldn't hire anyone in the department, S. took it upon himself to fill the role they needed, and it was a sacrifice on his part. But he did help both the department and me personally. Once, when we were really getting chewed up, he said to me, "No decision to close you down has been made."

the vodka. Some time later he left his position in the prosecutor's office and got a much less prestigious job as a legal advisor.

The men efficiently began to search the apartment. There were a lot of them, and they filled all three of our rooms. The first room, the biggest, was occupied by my library. My library had also seized the second room, which was our bedroom and Zara Grigorievna's study. And the third one was the children's room. Incidentally, in the children's room, the freshest product of ten-year-old Alyosha's romance games with his friend was lying on the table. His friend was the son of Riga-based Professor Sidyakov (he stayed with us practically all the time). Yura Sidyakov, who was engrossed by court romances and Dumas, had organized the "Society for the Physical Destruction of the Princes of Evil and the Enemies of Chivalry." At one point one of my guests solemnly brought me this piece of paper and in a most revolting voice demanded that I explain who organized this society, who was included in it, and what the goals of the society were. Incidentally, the appearance of the paper was so clearly childish—and among the guests there still turned out to be some not entirely devoid of reason—that the paper was not included in the protocol and, later on, did not figure in the case.

Meanwhile my guests were busy with their exceptionally painstaking and entirely unpromising labor. They had begun by taking book after book from the shelves and paging through each one, although this apparently soon bored them. I felt sick with anxiety waiting for them to get to Gorbanevskaya's manuscripts.

As for Zara Grigorievna, she was sitting at the table in this room full of unpleasant guests, calmly reading proofs. She was truly a stunningly brave person; I've never seen her frightened in my life.

It was getting dark. Zara Grigorievna, who was demonstratively, much more carefully than usual, maintaining our regular family life, got dinner together for me and the children. With hungry eyes, the KGB agents watched us having our supper in the middle of the crowd of them. Maybe this played a decisive role: when the only unsearched place that remained was the chimiiney where Gorbanevskaya's archive was, the chief muttered something not very printable which I will convey by the formula "there's nothing here," and he suggested that I sign a record of the proceedings, which I did only after they agreed to add a line stating that nothing forbidden had been found, and to provide a full list of confiscated papers (they had taken a typewriter and some typed copies of articles on semiotics that had already been published)[19].

They sealed up the cabinets they had overlooked. The cabinets remained sealed shut for months, after which a gentleman came by and, once he'd expressed himself with a most eloquent lexicon, simply took off the seals without even looking inside the cabinets. Basically the general impression was that this activity was terribly boring for them. The situation became typically Russian when my student's husband came by later and apologized until I got bored, and he finally suggested we have a drink.

Later I found out that they reported much less favorable results through their channels to the rector, and even included the formula that during the search they had confiscated documents of an anti-Soviet nature. As a consequence, I was issued a special provision in the Gorbanevskaya case, and this provision didn't quite merit its own "case," but also wasn't quite an acquittal. This legal complication followed me for a quite a while and, in part because of it, for a long time I was not allowed to travel abroad, even when all these reasons and all these bans ceased to be actively enforced.

Later, I burned the sheaf of papers, and I told Gorbanevskaya about it, but it didn't interest her at all: in a regular situation, there

---

19 There are actually two plots to this story. First of all, in addition to Gorbanevskaya's papers were their own—*Doctor Zhivago, The Fourth Prose,* some of Brodsky's poetry, and so on. (In Moscow all that would have been considered small potatoes, but in the provinces it was a great crime.) During the search my father calmly took them out from their various places, put them in his briefcase, and "went to work." Second of all, in addition to Gorbanevskaya, G. Superfin often stayed over in our second apartment, where my cousin Natasha lived after the death of my maternal aunt. Some of Superfin's papers were there, either abandoned or else forgotten. The search was conducted on the two apartments simultaneously, but the KGB guys in the second apartment behaved much more boldly. I can judge the care taken by those searching by the following detail: when I went to the completely wrecked apartment about a week later, I picked up the first piece of paper I came upon. It was a typewritten copy of the secret addendum to the Molotov-Ribbentrop Pact (I still have that paper). (Mikhail Lotman's note)

would not have been anything particularly criminal about those papers. It was known as forbidden literature, and this literature was supposed to be dispensed through various secure points among sympathizers. I think, to her romantic subconscious, it seemed that she had created a kind of emergency literary holding.

VII.

When we arrived in Tartu, the "Scholarly Proceedings" were practically never published. The single philological issue consisted in one purely subjective article by Adams on Gogol. The World Congress on Slavic Studies, conducted in the USSR for the first time in 1958 in Moscow, became the pretext under which we received Klement's permission to publish a whole volume. This was the first issue of the *Proceedings on Russian and Slavic Philology*, as we named our new series. At the same time I obtained permission for my monograph on the life and work of A. S. Kaisarov. This work took a lot of time and effort—well, better to say it didn't "take," but rather gave me many really happy moments. Thus began the Tartu publications on Slavic Studies.

The publication of the first volume of the *Proceedings* was motivated by the World Congress on Slavic Studies, but later (and here we must thank Rector Klement) we had to *de facto* earn the right to an annually published volume of the *Proceedings on Russian and Slavic Philology* for ourselves—and a significantly expanded volume at that. And after some time we got permission to found yet another independent series—a semiotic series which became one of our major life works; that is, Egorov's, Zara Grigorievna's, and mine.

For some reason, the word "semiotics" really worked our Moscow opponents up. Attacks against our school were carried out from two sides: first, we were accused of depoliticizing the sciences, and second, of dehumanizing them. In fact, our opponents often united their fronts, and in the articles of one and the same author, you could read that "the Tartu School is dehumanizing literary scholarship and dooming it to a lack of ideology." The centers of the "humanist" approach were the Moscow Institute of World Literature and the Soviet division of the Pushkin House.

We acted according to Krylov's principle: "They'll do their barking and then they'll leave us alone." Over my entire scholarly career, during which I have written and published several hundred works, I never once replied to any polemical attacks. This was done not from arrogance, of which I was accused more than once by my opponents, but because I always had to save time and paper. Zara Grigorievna, Boris Fedorovich, and I agreed on this principle: consider every issue as though it were the last. We always presumed the possibility of the complete annihilation of our publication. On the one hand, this led to a focused intensity of work, but on the other hand, the coordination of the issue's composition would sometimes be distorted. We would include writings which, in calmer conditions, could have been published separately.

In those years, scholarship was developing extremely quickly, especially in Moscow and Leningrad. In Moscow, a circle of young and very talented scholars cropped up around V. V. Ivanov. This was a kind of explosion, comparable only to cultural flashes like the Renaissance or the 18th century. And the very epicenter of the explosion wasn't Russian culture, but rather the study of Indian culture, or Eastern Studies in general, as well as Medieval Studies. There was a need for scholarly integration, but it wasn't easy to acheive. Tartu and Moscow came from different places and to a large extent were on different paths. Moscow in particular was based on linguistic research and the study of archaic forms of culture. Moreover, if folklore, and literature like detective fiction—that is, the genres that are oriented towards tradition and closed language—if these are considered the natural training ground for semiotics, then the possibility of applying semiotic methods to complex open systems, like modern art, was altogether subject to doubts.

During the first Summer School, I. I. Revzin and I had a very pointed discussion about this topic (in using the word "pointed," I want to evoke the intensity inherent in the pursuit of scholarly principles. This intensity never impeded the relations between us, relations which had been established immediately, relations of extraordinary warmth and respect—rather, this background of warmth made such intensity possible.). Revzin, a linguist of genius (I don't hesitate to use this term), died too early—that is, at the exact moment when he was on the brink of fundamentally new semiotic ideas. But during the first Summer School, he decidedly defended the inapplicability of semiotic methods to individual creativity, restricting them to folklore. The idea of an inseparable bond that exists between semiotic methods and closed traditional structures was later further developed by A. K. Zholkovsky and Yuri K. Shcheglov, and it led to their interest in detective fiction as a structure in which the laws of language significantly dominated the texts. Later, however, even these researchers focused their attention on the works of Ilf and Petrov. And when they had broadened the scope of their research, they turned a significant portion of their interests to the field of rule violations. However, in the beginning their interests were in the sphere of closed-text systems.

The direct collision of different schools—and, moreover, different scholars, who were distinguished by their individual scholarly features and their areas of expertise, more or less oriented towards either traditional or personal art—turned out to be quite fruitful, and the future development of semiotic research owes much to this happy combination.

The inclusion of B. M. Gasparov in the Tartu group, beginning in the third Summer School, further enriched the general movement, and so the principle of diversity within unity was confirmed clearly and anew.

I've already said that we were considering every new volume and every Summer School as our last. This is not a rhetorical statement. The scholarly movement was accomplished against the backdrop of a situation to which the words of Pasternak are relevant:

And in our days even the air smells of death:
To open a window is to open your veins.

Against this backdrop lay two cultural orientations. Gasparov presented one, which was to continue along the lines of Pasternak's directive: a closedness, a desire not to "open the window." The philosophy of the "ivory tower" was fundamental for Gasparov (which, incidentally, sharply contrasted with his talent as an excellent speaker who loved to and knew how to master his audience). But as for Zara Grigorievna, Boris Fedorovich, and myself, we became "enlighteners" as a matter of principle, and we sought to "sow the reasonable, the good, the eternal."

A snake sheds its skin when it grows. This is a perfect symbolic expression of scholarly progress. In order to stay true to itself, the process of cultural development should change sharply in its own time. The old skin gets too tight and doesn't protect well anymore; it hinders growth. The Tartu School and I both had to toss away our old skin several times throughout our scholarly lives. The closest example is the difficulties of its present state, as nearly the entire cast has changed, replenished with a new generation. And the older generation is noticeably disappearing from the scene. No matter how sad the individual moments of this process are, it is not only inevitable, but necessary. Moreover, it was as if we had programmed it beforehand. All that remains is to hope that the snake, having shed its skin, changed its color, and increased its size, will still preserve the very unity of itself.

I.

Voroshilov: Kliment Efremovich Voroshilov (1881-1969), a Soviet military commander and high-ranking member of the Politburo.

The Government Inspector: Nikolai Gogol's 1836 comedy in which Khlestakov, a foolish clerk, arrives in a small Russian town and is mistaken for an inspector come to investigate the local administration. In a 1975 essay entitled "On Khlestakov," Lotman analyzes him as a personality without imagination, which leads him to consume, rather than to generate, romanticism.[20] Lotman's Khlestakov sees that his own internal world is worthless, and is jealous of the alien world, the world of others, around him.

Lida: Lidiya Mikhailovna Lotman (1917-2011), Yuri Lotman's middle sister, a literary scholar in her own right.

Grigory Aleksandrovich Gukovsky: Gukovsky (1902-1950), a prominent literary scholar and a popular professor at Leningrad State University, was arrested during the campaign of anti-cosmopolitanism in Stalin's last years on a charge of "promoting bourgeois cosmopolitanism and formalism in their worst and most noxious sense," and died soon after his arrest in a Moscow prison.[21]

Ivan Ivanovich Tolstoy: Tolstoy (1880-1954) a classicist at Leningrad State University, also arrested under Stalin, allegedly for his relationship with the ABDEM group of philologists.[22]

Gnedich: Lotman published an encyclopedia article on Nikolai Ivanovich Gnedich (1784-1833), widely read translator of Homer into Russian, in 1964.

History of Russian Literature: This vast publication came out in volumes the size of phone books, each new volume spanning another

---

20 Lotman, Yuri M. "O Khlestakove." *Izbrannye stat'i v trekh tomakh. Tom I: Stat'i po semiotike i tipologii kul'tury.* Tallinn: Aleksandra, 1992. 337-364.

21 Azadovskii, Konstantin, and Boris Egorov. "From Anti-Westernism to Anti-Semitism." In *Journal of Cold War Studies.* Issue 4:1 (Winter 2002): 79.

22 Ibid., 79.

period of Russian literature.

Aleksandr Sergeevich: Also Pushkin's first name and patronymic.

Danilevsky: Grigory Petrovich Danilevsky (1829-1890), writer of historical fiction.

N. N. Ge: Nikolai Nikolaevich Ge (1831-1894), a realist painter known for his historical and religious works. *Pushkin at Mikhailovskoe* (1875) depicts a young Pushkin standing in the center of a living room, balancing on one leg, with one arm outstretched, reading aloud to an older couple.

Rykov: Aleksei Ivanovich Rykov (1881-1938) immediately succeeded Lenin as the head of the Soviet government in 1924, and was arrested and executed in 1938.

When Ribbentrop came to Moscow: Joachim Von Ribbentrop (1893-1946), the Foreign Minister of Germany throughout World War II, played a key role in the Treaty of Non-Aggression between Germany and the Soviet Union, which was signed during Ribbentrop's visit to Moscow in August 1939. This treaty came to be known as the Molotov-Ribbentrop Pact, and remained in effect until Hitler invaded the Soviet Union on June 22, 1941. In addition to the non-aggression pact, Molotov and Ribbentrop included a secret addendum stating that Germany would give the USSR the Baltic States. This addendum was not published in the USSR until 1989.

Partisan groups: The Soviet partisans, essentially groups of guerilla fighters during the war, were organized by the Soviet state to fight the German occupation of Soviet territory.

A Great Life: Russian "Большая жизнь." This 1939 film, directed by Leonid Lukov, treats the coal miners of the Donets Basin and won the Stalin Prize of the second order in 1941.

A Farewell to Arms: Hemingway's 1929 novel tells the story of a battlefield romance between an American Lieutenant and a British nurse against the backdrop of the Italian Campaigns of World War I.

International Literature: This journal, published monthly in Moscow from 1933 through 1943, showcased art, literature, and politics from overseas. *International Literature* began as the confluence of two separate journals, *The Herald of Foreign Literature* and *Literature of the World Revolution*, and resurfaced in 1955 under the name

Foreign Literature, hence Lotman's confusion over its title.

Blok's *The Twelve:* This apocalyptic 1918 poem by Aleksandr Blok treats the October Revolution of 1917, likening the Bolshevik soldiers of the Revolution to the Twelve Apostles.

Mark Konstantinovich Azadovsky: Azadovsky (1888-1954) held the chair of folklore studies at Leningrad State University during Stalin's anti-cosmopolitan campaign, was targeted along with Gukovsky and several other leading academics and intellectuals of the time. Azadovsky in particular was denounced as a "standard-bearer of the ideas of cosmopolitanism who mercilessly slandered the great Russian poet Pushkin," apparently for his suggestions that Pushkin may have drawn some of his literary influences from the West.[23]

Vladimir Yakovlevich Propp: The world-renowned author of *Morphology of the Folktale* (1928), Propp (1895-1970) taught at Leningrad State University from 1932 until his death.

Kirza boots: Made of artificial leather invented in the Soviet Union in 1935, these boots were produced en masse for Soviet soldiers in the early 1940s.

If Tomorrow Brings War: Russian "Если завтра война." Directed by Efim Dzigan and released in 1938, this documentary won the Stalin Prize of the second order in 1941 and treats the Red Army preparing for combat. The lyrics Lotman quotes in Russian are "Если завтра война, / Если враг нападет, / Если тучею черной нагрянет . . ."

All Quiet on the Western Front: This 1929 novel by Erich Maria Remarque describes the German front line experiences during World War I.

Kolkhoz: An abbreviation of kollektivnoe khoziaistvo, the Russian for "collective farm."

Kutaisi: Lotman's war itinerary began with Leningrad; moved to Kutaisi, Georgia, when he was drafted in the fall of 1940; on to Shepetovka and Yuzvin, in Ukraine, just before Germany invaded; then to the Mogilyov-Podolsky area, where Romania bordered Ukraine on the banks of the Dniester, as war broke out in June 1941. From the Dniester his unit retreated to the Don River in the summer

23 Ibid., 79.

of 1942, still in Ukraine; and then further East to the Mozdok area, on the Terek River, in Ingushetia. In 1943 they moved West again, to the Donets Basin in Ukraine; and then in the spring of 1944 still further West in Ukraine, where Lotman's unit was stationed when the war ended.

Budyonny: Marshal Semyon Mikhailovich Budyonny (1883-1973) was a civil war hero and Soviet military commander.

Timoshenko: Semyon Konstantinovich Timoshenko (1895-1970) succeeded Voroshilov as People's Commissar for Defense for a year, and was himself succeeded by Stalin.

Arakcheev: Count Aleksei Andreevich Arakcheev (1769-1834), a general under Tsars Paul I and Alexander I, known for his brutality. His name has come to stand for a repressive military state.

Extended the phone lines: Lotman was a battery telephonist for his army unit, meaning that he was responsible for setting up and taking down the coils of phone lines wherever his unit set up camp.

Full freedom: The word I have translated "freedom" is not the usual word for freedom, *svoboda*, but rather *volia*, a word suggesting a more existential and nearly anarchic freedom. Ozhegov's dictionary offers "the condition of freedom" [*svobodnoe sostoianie*] as a definition for this word.

Three days before the war . . . the 19th: Germany broke the Molotov-Ribbentrop Pact and invaded the USSR on June 22, 1941.

Pushkin's Salieri: Lotman quotes from Aleksandr Pushkin's verse drama *Mozart and Salieri*, published in 1830. The lines in Russian are: "Как будто тяжкий совершил я долг, / Как будто нож целебный мне отсек / Страдавший член!"

"Scram": Russian драпать. This verb, which Lotman uses continuously throughout the text, starts out tongue-in-cheek and gradually loses its irony as he begins to drop the quotation marks surrounding it, and as he employs more military slang. It suggests fleeing in shame, and Lotman often uses it instead of the word *otstuplenie* ("retreat"), a much more formal synonym.

Barbusse: Author of the pacifist novel *Under Fire* (1916), which treats experience in the French Army during World War I, Henri Barbusse (1873-1935) was a communist and friend to the USSR.

"Junkers": A German aircraft manufacturer. Lotman mentions two types of plane specifically: a Junkers 87 and a Junkers 88. Both were designed in 1935 as bomber planes. The 87 was a two-man ground-attack plane, and the more versatile 88 twin-engine aircraft was used as a dive-bomber, night fighter, reconnaissance engine, and torpedo bomber.

Heinkel aircraft: Another German aircraft manufacturer and provider of bomber planes to the German air force during the war.

II.

Tvardovsky: Aleksandr Trifonovich Tvardovsky (1910-1971), poet and editor of the journal *New World* (1950-1954, 1958-1970), published his war poem *Vasily Tyorkin* serially from 1941-1945. The poem depicts a soldier on the Eastern Front during the Second World War and won Tvardovsky the Stalin Prize in 1946.

Oistrakh: David Fedorovich Oistrakh (1908-1974), renowned classical violinist.

Hašek: Jaroslav Hašek (1883-1923), Czech anarchist and member of the Bolshevik party, author of the humorous war novel *The Good Soldier Švejk.*

Order of the Red Star: An order bestowed by the Soviet Union upon army and navy officers for exceptional service. The order physically consisted of an enameled red star with a soldier engraved in the middle, and was worn on the chest of its bearer.

IV.

Tolstoy wrote . . . : From the 1857 novella *Lucerne*. The part Lotman mentions comes from the end, as the narrator-protagonist ruminates on the events of the day.

As Speransky said to Baten'kov . . . : Count Mikhail Mikhailovich Speransky (1772-1839), liberal advisor to Tsar Alexander I, worked closely with writer and Decembrist Gavriil Stepanovich Baten'kov (1793-1863) on the Code of Siberia, a political endeavor designed to reform the system of government in the Siberian regions.

Fadeev: In his capacity as a major literary official, novelist Aleksandr Aleksandrovich Fadeev (1901-1956) participated in Stalin's anti-cosmopolitan campaigns and killed himself when Khrushchev "revealed" the abuses of the Stalinist regime. Kornei Chukovsky, a well-known critic and children's poet of the time, wrote in his diary how sorry he was upon hearing of Fadeev's suicide:

> An essentially decent human being who loved literature "to tears" had ended by steering the ship of literature into the most perilous, most shameful of waters and attempting to combine humaneness with the secret-police mentality. Hence the zigzags in his behavior, hence the tortured conscience of his final years. He wasn't born to be a loser; he was so accustomed to being a leader, the arbiter of writers' fates, that having to withdraw from the position of literary marshal was agony for him.[24]

Karamzin: Lotman began publishing on Karamzin in 1952, and his work on the historian and writer culminated in the monograph *The Creation of Karamzin (Sotvorenie Karamzina*, 1987).

Attacks on Eikhenbaum: Along with Gukovsky and Azadovsky, Boris Mikhailovich Eikhenbaum (1886-1959) was targeted during Stalin's anti-cosmopolitan campaigns. During the "assessment," Eikhenbaum was accused of "kowtowing to the West," of "using a comparativist methodology," and of waging an "anti-patriotic campaign to destroy the national distinctiveness of great Russian writers."[25]

---

24 Chukovskii, Kornei. *Diary, 1901-1969*. Eds. Erlich, Victor, and Michael Henry Heim. New Haven: Yale University Press, 2005. 406.

25 Azadovskii and Egorov, 79.

Macbeth: The quoted lines take place in Act I, Scene III, spoken by Banquo to Macbeth of the three witches.

Zhirmunsky: Along with Gukovsky, Azadovsky, and Eikhenbaum, Viktor Maksimovich Zhirmunsky (1891-1971) was the fourth professor to be targeted during the particularly severe attacks made on the Leningrad State University professors by Stalin's anti-cosmopolitan campaigns. Zhirmunsky was the chair of the department of Western European Literature and was accused during the assessment of "disparaging Russian literature's accomplishments" and "speaking like a devoted mystic and a German Idealist."[26]

"Knolls and brooks": A piece of a quote from Khlestakov in Gogol's *The Government Inspector,* addressing the mayor's daughter. The dialogue runs as follows:

> ANNA ANDREEVNA: . . . You honor me too much. I don't deserve it.
>
> KHLESTAKOV: Whyever don't you deserve it? Madam, you do deserve it.
>
> ANNA ANDREEVNA: I live in the country . . .
>
> KHLESTAKOV: Well, the country, however, also has its knolls, its brooks . . .

Pushkin House: Established in 1905, the Institute of Russian Literature (familiarly called the Pushkin House) was hit particularly hard during Stalin's anti-cosmopolitan campaigns. Leading scholars and public intellectuals employed by this institution were castigated and fired, while anti-intellectual members of Stalin's government took their places.

Berdnikov: Georgy Petrovich Berdnikov (1915-1996), in addition to the political career path that Lotman outlines, was also a literary scholar and taught at Leningrad State University. Lotman is unforgiving in his descriptions of this man, but he has omitted Berdnikov's worst personal offenses. He makes clear that Berdnikov owed his acadmic career to Gukovsky, who helped him considerably during a time of financial need, but does not make clear that Berdnikov himself presided cruelly over Gukovsky's "assessment", and was in large part responsible for his (and Zhirmunsky's, and Azadovsky's, and

---

26 Ibid., 79.

Eikhenbaum's) tragic fate. Berdnikov reappeared later in Lotman's life to lead a political campaign against Tartu specifically. Despite Berdnikov's villainous role in the lives and careers of Lotman and his mentors, the two did remain in correspondance throughout their adult lives. A 1982 postcard from Berdnikov announces his pleasure at reading Lotman's latest book and mentions his fond memories of Lotman as a youth. It is not clear whether Berdnikov ever read *Non-Memoirs* when they were published in 1995, but he was certainly still alive at the time of Lotman's dictating these stories.

Fedya Abramov: Fedor Aleksandrovich Abramov (1920-1983), novelist and short story writer.

Fifth paragraph: A line in the Russian passport designating ethnicity.

Pnin: An article by Lotman on poet and critic Ivan Petrovich Pnin (1773-1805) was finally published in 1964.

Abakumov: Viktor Semenovich Abakumov (1908-1954), the notoriously brutal Soviet security chief, was arrested in 1951 and condemned to death by military tribunal in 1954.

Komsomol: An abbreviation of *Kommunisticheskii soyuz molodyozhi,* "Communist Union of Youth."

Tynianov's novella: Yuri Tynianov's (1894-1943) 1927 novella *Lieutenant Kizhe,* about a bureaucratic error resulting in the creation of a phantom lieutenant, relies on a Russian phonological pun: a clerk accidentally writes "Podporuchik Kizhe" [Lieutenant Kizhe] instead of "podporuchiki zhe" [. . . now, as for lieutenants], thus writing a phantom into existence. The story follows the chimerical lieutenant through promotions, marriage, a good reputation with the emperor, and finally an honorable death.

Maksimov: Dmitry Evgen'evich Maksimov (1904-1987), the academic mentor of Zara Mints, was a scholar of Russian Symbolism.

Blok: Aleksandr Aleksandrovich Blok (1880-1921) was a leading Symbolist poet.

"The men of the '40s": Berdnikov is invoking the great liberal intellectuals of the 1840s. The irony of Lotman's decision to include this story lies in how drastically and brutally Berdnikov's career broke with the values of political and literary liberalism represented by "the men of the '40s," the first definitive cohort in the tradition of

Russian intelligentsia.

Bilinkis: Yakov Semenovich Bilinkis (1926-2001) was a scholar of Russian literature, particularly of Tolstoy.

"Build socialism in one classroom": A humorous reference to the Stalinist slogan about "building socialism in one country," publicized by Nikolai Bukharin in his 1925 brochure *Can We Build Socialism in One Country in the Absence of the Victory of the West-European Proletariat?*

"The tragedy of the circumstances": The Sovieticization of Estonia, annexed in 1940, and reoccupied in 1944, was accompanied by massive political repressions against the native population.

Misha: Mikhail Yurevich Lotman (born 1952), Yuri Lotman's eldest son, a scholar of semiotics and a politician in Estonia.

Adams: Valmar (Vladimir Karlovich) Adams (1899–1993), a scholar of Russian literature and an Estonian poet, was arrested in 1951 and spent more than three years in jail and labor camps. After his return to Tartu, he taught in the Department of Russian literature.

Intuitionism: In his 1964 *Lektsii po struktural'noi poetike*, Lotman states that "intuitionism is a generic term for a number of idealistic philosophical studies of an anti-intellectual persuasion—studies that consider intuitive knowledge to be higher and more scientific than scientific—that is, experimental and logical—knowledge."[27]

---

27 Lotman, Iurii. *Lektsii po struktural'noi poetike. Vyp.1 (Vvedenie, teoriia stikha).* Uchenye zapiski Tartuskogo gosudarstvennogo universiteta, vyp. 160. *Trudy po zankovym sistemam, [vyp.] 1).* Tartu, 1964. 34.

V.

Solzhenitsyn: Aleksandr Isaevich Solzhenitsyn (1918-2008) published *One Day in the Life of Ivan Denisovich* in 1962.

Elena Sergeevna Bulgakova: Bulgakova (1893-1970), wife of renowned author Mikhail Bulgakov, was a close friend of Lotman and Mints.

Simonov: Konstantin Mikhailovich Simonov (1915-1979), poet and editor-in-chief of the literary journals *Novii Mir* [New World] and *Literaturnaya Gazeta* [Literary Gazette] 1946-1950 and then again 1954-1958, and 1950-1953 respectively. As the secretary of the Union of Writers of the USSR 1946-1959 and 1967-1979, helped publish Bulgakov's *Master and Margarita* serially in 1966-1967, and wrote the introduction to the first single-volume edition in 1967.

Svidrigailov and Marmeladov: Depraved characters in Dostoevsky's 1866 novel *Crime and Punishment*.

VI.

Natalya Gorbanevskaya: Natalya Evgen'evna Gorbanevskaya (1936-2013), a poet and translator, was imprisoned and institutionalized for her role as editor of the *Chronicle of Current Events*, the primary dissident publication in the Soviet Union.

VII.

Kaisarov: Lotman's monograph on the poet Andrei Sergeevich Kaisarov (1782-1813) was published in 1962.

Krylov: Ivan Andreevich Krylov (1769-1844), Russia's leading fabulist and founder of the satirical magazine *Pochta dukhov* [The Spirits' Mail], on which Lotman published an article in 1958.

V. V. Ivanov: Viacheslav Vsevolodovich Ivanov, born 1929, the primary figure around whom the "Moscow" end of the Moscow-Tartu School of semiotics developed.

Summer School: Inspired by Ivanov's academic symposia in Moscow, Lotman and his colleagues established a tradition of semiotic-themed conventions in Tartu called the Summer School of Semiotics in August 1964.

Pasternak: Boris Pasternak's 1918 poem in full:

> Рояль дрожащий пену с губ оближет.
> Тебя сорвет, подкосит этот бред.
> Ты скажешь: - милый! – Нет, - вскричу я – нет!
> При музыке? – Но можно ли быть ближе,
>
> Чем в полутьме, аккорды, как дневник,
> Меча в камин комплектами, погодно?
> О пониманье дивное, кивни,
> Кивни и изумишься! – ты свободна.
>
> Я не держу. Иди, благотвори.
> Ступай к другим. Уже написан Вертер,
> А в наши дни и воздух пахнет смертью.
> Открыть окно что жилы отворить.[28]

---

28 Pasternak, Boris L. *Stikhotvoreniia i poemy*. Ed. Siniavskii, A., and Lev Ozerov. Leningrad: Sovetskii pisatel', 1965. 176-177.

The trembling piano licks the foam from its lips.
This delirium will break you, cut you down.
You'll say, "Darling!" "No," I'll cry out, "No!
In the presence of music?" But could we be closer

Than this: tossing chords at dusk, like a diary,
Into the fireplace—volume by volume, year by year?
Oh, miraculous understanding, nod yes,
Nod yes and you're amazed—you're free.

I do not keep you. Go on, do good.
Go to the others. Werther has already been written.
And in our days even the air smells of death:
To open a window is to open your veins.

"To sow the good, the reasonable, the eternal": A line from Nikolai
Nekrasov's 1876 poem, "To the Sowers," reproduced below in full:

СЕЯТЕЛЯМ
Сеятель знанья на ниву народную!
Почву ты, что ли, находишь бесплодную,
    Худы ль твои семена?
Робок ли сердцем ты? слаб ли ты силами?
Труд награждается всходами хилыми,
    Доброго мало зерна!
Где же вы, умелые, с бодрыми лицами,
Где же вы, с полными жита кошницами?
Труд засевающих робко, крупицами,
    Двиньте вперед!
Сейте разумное, доброе, вечное,
Сейте! Спасибо вам скажет сердечное
    Русский народ . . .[29]

---

29 Nekrasov, Nikolai A. *Sochineniia v trekh tomakh*: v. 2. Moscow: Gosudarstven-
noe izdatel'stvo khudozhestvennoi literatury, 1959. 288.

TO THE SOWERS

Sower of knowledge in the people's field!
Do you find the soil fruitless, or is it that
        Your seeds are lean?
Are you shy of heart? Are you weak in spirit?
Your work is rewarded with stunted shoots,
        Your grains of little good!
Wherever are you, able ones, with your spry faces,
Wherever are you, with your baskets full of wheat?
The work has been sown shyly, seed by seed—
        Strike forward!
Sow the reasonable, the good, the eternal,
Sow! You will be thanked from the heart
        Of the Russian people . . .

IN MAY 1985, on the occasion of the V-Day anniversary, Tartu students were invited to a lecture hall meeting with their two professors, Pavel Reifman and Yuri Lotman, both distinguished scholars of Russian literature, who shared their personal memories of being soldiers in the last war. Among the episodes that Lotman told that day were some that would later become parts of *Non-Memoirs*: Lotman enthusiastically drew pictures of the front line lice-exterminating barrels on the chalkboard, and shocked his students with the observation that the actual experience of combat is less frightening than imagining or remembering it. Even during this public performance, Lotman's memories of the war were already well-structured: engrossing and eloquent public speaking was second nature to this master lecturer and famously brilliant raconteur, but it was also clear that Lotman had had many opportunities to polish his war stories among family, friends, and colleagues.

Lotman's artistry in *Non-Memoirs* resides in his role as a raconteur. This world-renowned semiotician and cultural historian—one of the greatest intellectuals produced by the Soviet Union—was also a craftsman of the anecdote. In his memoirs, the apparent simplicity of the "war story" genre dovetails with the levels of complexity that constitute his narration. And yet Lotman's stories feel familiar to his listeners even as he recounts experiences of estrangement and uncanniness.

Familiarity can make it hard to recognize the mastery of his craftsmanship. There's not much remove: reading these memoirs, we might be in his kitchen, drinking tea with him and listening to his stories—much as his students, colleagues, friends and family did, much as his assistant Jelena Pogosjan did while transcribing this very document. Of course, this storytelling is its own genre; our familiarity and Lotman's jokes and digressions are some of its characteristic features. But it is a pleasure to find that in *Non-Memoirs*, his voice often gleams with conversational warmth, with the wit of a well-timed punchline, occasional profanities, and exclamations of delight.

But the ease of our experience reading these memoirs is in dialogue with their complexity. Lotman's stories bear up to scrutiny—and often demand it—on myriad levels, yielding history, historiography, literature, culture, politics, and semiotics to the careful and curious reader. In part, they're complex because of who Lotman is—heir to the Russian Formalists and to a generation of Pushkin scholars, pioneer of semiotic and cultural studies, this great literary biographer problematizes his own situation as autobiographer throughout. They're further complicated by Lotman's rigorous commitment to detailed description of certain elements of his experience—the tasks of a battery telephonist, the semiotics of front line slang, the exact empty feeling of anguish after the war ended but before the troops were demobilized—and the corollary to those details, his enigmatic elusiveness (or is it merely discretion?) on other matters, matters where the political meets the personal. These memoirs are complex, too, because of how much Lotman borrows from other literary conventions—the greatest example of which is the Tolstoyan tradition—and how much he alters. How rarely he moralizes, even against these backdrops of combat and political repression, settings rich with moral concerns—and how effective it is when he does. Complex, finally, for generic reasons: are they memoirs or not?

During a January 2012 interview in Tartu, scholar Ljubov Kisseljova—Lotman's student and longtime colleague—discussed the import of the prefix "Non-" in Lotman's title for his memoirs. "He didn't think of it as a completed text," Kisseljova remarked.[30] The challenges presented by biography in general, specifically literary biography, layered with the distinctly Lotmanian problems of writing oneself into history post-factum, are suggested by this prefix of negation, this first unit of meaning in the entire document. The uncertain structure of the narrative as a whole—the very history of the text—also reflects the problems of autobiography and the right to a role in history. The reader of *Non-Memoirs* is in a strange position indeed: in reading Lotman we do not encounter him alone. His reader must engage with his self-as-narrator, with his self-as-protagonist, with his editors and publishers (some of whom are also actors in the

---

30 Interview with Ljubov Kisseljova, January 18, 2012.

memoirs), with those who first listened to his war stories and with those who transcribed him, with his translator, and with the vast community of others reading him, interpreting him, and committing him to memory.

These problems all lead to larger questions haunting the text, both in the content of its stories and the history of its creation. What is the relationship between event and narrative in history? Can an individual claim authorship? What is the function of memory in historiography? *Non-Memoirs* continues along the path of Lotman's latest theoretical and critical writings, invoking a community of authors whose intentions and languages sometimes accord, sometimes clash, and thus produce a vibrant culture, or a living text. "There is a constant exchange, a search for a common language, a *koine*, and creolized semiotic systems come into being," writes Lotman in *On the Semiosphere* (1984), in a discussion of the role of the "boundary" in language and culture. "Even in order to wage war there has to be a common language."[31] Thus, as the Lotmanian model of culture is established from the constant dialogue and communication between languages within the semiosphere, much like the interactions and clashes between armies on shifting national borders during wartime, so is literature dependent on a community and a variety of readers and authors, and so is history on a jostling collective memory.[32]

* * *

Isaak Babel's *Red Cavalry* cycle (*Konarmiia*, 1926) made manifest the traditional narrative of a very young, deeply civilian man going to war and attempting to gain a proper, soldierly masculinity. One version of this archetypal story—as we find in Babel's war cycle—is the narrower trope of the physically weak, overly intellectual Jewish youth either about to go to war or already on the front, and stepping onto the path to manhood. He encounters and must overcome some

---

31 Lotman, Yuri. *Universe of the Mind: A Semiotic Theory of Culture.* Trans. Ann Shukman. Bloomington: Indiana University Press, 1990. 142.

32 Lotman, Yuri. *Culture and Explosion.* Ed. Marina Grishakova. Trans. Wilma Clark, Berlin: Mouton de Gruyton, 2009. 6.

form of anti-Semitism. He learns to cultivate a warrior's body and a warrior's sensibility. We see him undergo rites of passage and pitfalls. His mentors and teachers in these steps toward maturation are his fellow soldiers and commanding officers; they are fraternal figures of envy and paternal figures of authority; they guide him (or shame him) along the road to manhood.

This particular narrative is all but absent in Lotman's *Non-Memoirs*. The question of his Jewishness on the front merits two sentences in a footnote. The message is clear: occasions of pre-war and front line anti-Semitism do not merit this memoirist's rigorous treatment. Neither do the traces of the Holocaust recently inflicted on the former Pale of Settlement; Lotman never touches upon this theme, although many other Jews who served in the Red Army recorded and reported their complete and utter shock at the scale of the devastation. For Lotman, however, this topic was either too traumatic or not easily enough squared with his carefully constructed young self.

An atmosphere of post-war anti-Semitism, however, is vividly rendered in *Non-Memoirs*. "Before the war, of course, nothing of the kind [i.e., anti-Semitic conduct] took place," Lotman maintains, proposing that anti-Semitism was culturally imported to the Soviet Union during the war—which is further supported by the occurrence of discrimination against Jews in Lotman's life only upon the end of the war, as he searches for employment and cannot find any. After the war, after demobilization, Lotman comes back from the front anti-climactically, in the middle of the night. No fanfare, no flowers, no crying girls are waiting to greet him—which Lotman notes with irony. He makes his way back to his childhood home by hitching a ride with an ambulance. His family has not waited up for him; no one has been informed of the date or time of his arrival. The next few months portrayed in *Non-Memoirs* make it clear how confused young Lotman is by the political climate of postwar Leningrad. How young he seems in the portrait he paints of himself, thirsty to spend days at a time in the stacks of the Public Library, unable to understand the brutal attacks on his mentor Boris Eikhenbaum, unable to fathom the fear overwhelming his teachers. "Somehow the seriousness of these attacks didn't reach my consciousness," he writes. During the war, "under specific formulaic circumstances, we had unmistakably known what we had to do to be honorable people. But now we found ourselves in entirely different circumstances—for which we didn't have any kind of clichéd formulae." There is very little in his self-portrait of these months to recommend any genre of new-found martial manhood in Lotman. This unstable moment in history marks the commencement of his journey to manhood—rather than its culmination.

The beginning of the delayed maturation narrative in *Non-Memoirs* coincides with the somewhat belated awakening of a sense of cultural Jewishness in the young, unemployed Lotman. The anti-Semitism he encounters in this story is not on the front lines, but in the academic job market during Stalin's campaign "against cosmopolitanism." His foes are not the Cossacks of Babel's *Red Cavalry*, but the thugs of Stalin's purges. His trials include having to move away from home to prove himself as a scholar and teacher in Tartu. His successes in his journey to masculinity are the securing of academic employment, the establishment of an intellectual and cultural network in the margins of the USSR, and the founding of a great research school in spite of all odds.

Lotman's delayed experience of anti-Semitism corresponds to his delayed account of entering into a community of masculinity. In what Lotman himself might call *minus priem*, or the narrative device marked by "meaningful absence," this community of masculinity (complete with rites of passage, father-figure mentors, and protagonist's successes) is not recognizably portrayed on the front lines, but instead is comprised of a tradition of academics; more specifically, Pushkin scholars.[33]

Lotman's own work on Pushkin began to see print as early as 1953, barely three years after he was settled in Tartu. In his essay "Double Portrait," which he dictated in 1992 and intended to publish

---

33 For more on the nineteenth- and twentieth-century tradition of Jews' success in the field of Pushkin studies, see Yuri Slekzine, *The Jewish Century* (Princeton, 2006), 127-128. Slezkine calls this phenomenon a "conversion to the Pushkin faith" and finds it to be widespread among Russian and Soviet intellectuals of Jewish extraction.

alongside *Non-Memoirs*, he sketches the personalities of his two professors and academic mentors Boris Tomashevsky and Grigory Gukovsky—both powerhouses in the field of Pushkin scholarship. In his description of Tomashevsky in particular, Lotman emphasizes the strength of the "masculine aura" surrounding his role models:

> One could continue the list of his various scholarly capabilities and interests, but upon personal acquaintance with him, one was struck not only by this list, but by a phenomenon more difficult to explain—that complex of noble, masculine qualities comprising the charm of the loftier timbre of the military man . . . If there exists some quintessence of the positive attributes of an authentic *man*, then this quintessence was manifest in Tomashevsky perhaps to a greater extent than any of the thousand men I've met in my lifetime . . . An atmosphere of masculinity dominated the allure of his mind—which was given to mockery—and his enormous erudition.[34]

The traits that condemned this type under Stalin's anti-cosmopolitan campaign—scholastic aptitude, intellectualism, and devotion to learning—also enabled depth and innovation in scholarship. Lotman's "Double Portrait" is a character sketch of one specific man and yet it serves as a convincing portrait of the league of senior scholars that welcomed him as one of their own: where inheritance and rite of passage are handed down neither from father to son, nor in battle, but largely from professor to student, subject to scholar, mentor to mentee.[35]

* * *

Lotman's *Non-Memoirs* reinvent two established narrative genres of Soviet war discourse: one oral, one literary. The oral genre with

34 Iu. M. Lotman, "Dvoinoi portret," *Lotmanovskii sbornik*, Moscow, 1995. www.ruthenia.ru/lotman/mem1/Lotman2portret.html (accessed October 5, 2012).

35 For more on figures of Jewish masculinity, see Daniel Boyarin, *Unheroic Conduct: The Rise of Heterosexuality and the Invention of the Jewish Man* (Berkeley, 1997), and Harry Brod, *A Mensch Among Men: Explorations in Jewish Masculinity* (Freedom, CA, 1988).

which Lotman worked was that of "war veterans reminiscing" (*veterany vspominaiut*) or perhaps even "lessons of courage" (*uroki muzhestva*), as they were also known to Soviet youth (the Russian *muzhestvo* also denotes "fortitude" and "virility"). This genre originated from the authorities' ideologically all-important belief that the country's victory in the Great Patriotic War was a historic achievement of the Soviet system, therefore adding legitimacy and permanence to the communist rule. The state invested enormous propagandistic and educational effort in persuading Soviet masses—especially youth—that by mobilizing the country's resources and guiding the people throughout the war years, the party-state system virtually created the victory. As an official commemorative practice, war veterans were encouraged to visit educational institutions, meet with young people, and treat them to stories of war heroism. These meetings were thought to help build Soviet patriotic spirit among the young. This was the standard formula for such presentations, but in reality, veterans would often digress from the edifying narrative scheme: instead of focusing on examples of characteristically Soviet bravery, they chose to relate their own deeply personal stories, rich in the emotional memories of wartime loss and hardship.

Intellectually invested in questions of historical psychology, Lotman was not averse to bringing up his observations of wartime human behavior in his university lectures on cultural theory and history. But it was at the somewhat formal commemorative meeting with the Tartu philological students that Lotman's war stories were aired possibly for the first time as a structured oral narrative. Both in his oral presentation and in *Non-Memoirs*, Lotman turned the officious Soviet genre of reminiscing about the war on its head: instead of inspirational examples of martial bravery, his war stories are both sharply analytical and entertaining, as he focuses on front line daily routines and the emotional universe of the soldiers, maintaining a neutral and intellectual but, at the same time, lively and ironic narrative tone. Speaking about soldiers' war experiences with a good deal of irony and minimal pathos had a celebrated precedent in Aleksandr Tvardovsky's wartime narrative poem *Vasily Tyorkin*, serialized in the newspaper *Red Army Truth* (*Krasnoarmeiskaia Pravda*) to enormous success among the military rank and file. Lotman never tired of declaring *Tyorkin* a work of genius and the most authentic reflection of soldiers' war labor. Indeed, he even cites *Tyorkin* in *Non-Memoirs*: both as an authority on body lice and as an example of heroic gunmanship that Lotman himself could never quite manage. Yet despite their occasional thematic and even tonal similarities, *Non-Memoirs* stands very far from Tvardovsky's poetic masterpiece. The poet explored the war path of Tyorkin, a peasant-turned-soldier, in folkloric idiom. Full of affection for the peasant's sly wisdom and innate patriotism, Tvardovsky constructed a poetic and rhetorical world that was profoundly different from Lotman's unabashedly intellectual and literary one.

To find literary parallels to *Non-Memoirs*, it may be more productive to look at another classic of Soviet war literature, Viktor Nekrasov's *In the Trenches of Stalingrad* (V okopakh Stalingrada). In his 1946 autobiographical novella, Nekrasov relates the experiences of a young intellectual who serves as an engineering officer in the battle of Stalingrad. For this book, Nekrasov was awarded the Stalin Prize in 1947 and thus, paradoxically, *In the Trenches of Stalingrad* became canonized before the Soviet canon of war writing was conceived. Nekrasov's books were withdrawn from Soviet libraries after 1973, when he became a political émigré. However, for the next thirteen years he remained a regular presence in the lives of many members of the Soviet intelligentsia as a popular commentator broadcasting from Radio Liberty's Paris studio. In his radio journalism, Nekrasov continually returned to his war experiences, the material of his first and most famous work.

While Nekrasov's Stalingrad novella is certainly not a straightforward memoir (and it is narrated in the present tense, emphasizing the immediacy of the events), this exceptional piece of Soviet war writing shares a number of motifs with Lotman's memoirs. Taking as its premise a young architect's adjustment to the physical and mental hardship of war, Nekrasov's autobiographical story uses a deliberately unemotional, factual, almost technical language, full of professional terms of military engineering and a good deal of soldiers' lingo (e.g., it features the expressions *drapat'* [rendered in *Non-Memoirs* as "scram"] and *spikirovat'* ["steal away"], both discussed semiotically by Lotman). Nekrasov pays great attention to the everyday routine of life and military labor in the trenches: from lice to drinking, bureaucracy, the shame of chaotic retreat, and the waste of soldiers' lives by incompetent commanders. Instead of demonstrating any passionate hatred of the Germans, the first-person narrator describes the labor involved in fighting the generalized "enemy." While Western antiwar fiction may have influenced Nekrasov's narrative style, his story is not a pacifist work *per se*: the sense of warm patriotism that animates the soldiers' quiet heroism is so present for him that it does need to be amplified with rhetorical flourishes. Nekrasov describes the daily horrors of the "just war" with a tone of suppressed emotion and cultured detachment, quite at odds with the pathos that would later be expected from a Soviet war writer by the conventions of official Soviet discourse.

* * *

Lidiya Ginzburg begins her *Notes of a Blockade Person* (*Zapiski blokadnogo cheloveka*, 1984), a collection of autobiographical and analytical notes on the siege of Leningrad, with a famous reference to Tolstoy's *War and Peace*. "During the war years," she writes, "people avidly read *War and Peace* in order to confirm their own experiences [*chtoby proverit' sebia*] (never to verify Tolstoy, whose authority no one doubted). And the reader would say to himself: Well, okay, I'm feeling this correctly. Okay, that means it's true."[36] This pronouncement would become a touchstone for Ginzburg's generation of Russian writers. By invoking Tolstoy and his absolute acuity in wartime psychology, as well as articulating the phenomenon of art verifying life ("not the other way around") during the surreality of war, Ginzburg had placed her finger on a quality common to the Soviet literary experience of war, both at home and on the front. Indeed, one finds references to Tolstoy throughout Soviet war fiction, from

---

36 Ginzburg, Lidiia. *"Zapiski blokadnogo cheloveka," Prokhodiashchie kharaktery. Proza voennykh let. Zapiski blokadnogo cheloveka.* Ed. Emily Van Buskirk and Andrei Zorin. Moscow: Novoe izdatel'stvo, 2011. 311.

emulating the entire epic genre of Tolstoy's *War and Peace* in Vasily Grossman's *For a Just Cause* (*Za pravoe delo*, 1952) and especially *Life and Fate* (*Zhizn' i sud'ba*, 1961) to Viktor Nekrasov's seemingly casual reference to Tolstoy's view of collective patriotism as a force that unconsciously animates Russian soldiers' perseverance.

Lotman chose to invoke Tolstoy very early in his *Non-Memoirs*, establishing him as one of the thematic voices governing the narrative: "I read *War and Peace* several times," he says, adding parenthetically, "(I still read it continuously, and I don't know how many times I've read it through—I probably know it by heart)." Informed by Tolstoy's own combat experiences during the 1854-1855 siege of Sevastopol, *War and Peace* can be considered not only a historical novel and a great iteration of Tolstoy's treatment of wartime psychology, but also one of his many attempts at autobiographical writing.

For Tolstoy, the varied psychologies, actions, and revelations of the characters in his war writing are all contingent on this fact: that war is murder, that to depict battlefield combat is to depict an inevitable moral compromise. In Lotman, this moral landscape is obscured by a semiotic one. For him, war writing is set in a landscape rich with signification, and the semiotic category, like Tolstoy's moral category, cannot be overcome.

Lotman refrains from expressing a Tolstoyan interest in the delicate liminal space between life and death. Tolstoy, famously interested in what is *revealed* at war, wrote in "Sevastopol in December" of soldiers' "other and higher" motivation in battle; in "Sevastopol in May," of the dying soldier's petty shame at unpaid debts, the futile hope to boast of bravery. In *Non-Memoirs*, Lotman also depicts behavior both honorable and shameful, but in doing so, he locates it within the "sign systems" underlying the war experience. Like Tolstoy's men, Lotman's cast of characters in the wartime sections of his memoirs are neither heroes nor martyrs; they're regular men in extreme circumstances. Like Tolstoy, Lotman's project centers on emphasizing grim and gritty conditions both physical and psychological. But for Tolstoy, the soldiers' "conditions of constant toil, lack of sleep, and dirt" either reveal or interrogate a universal spiritual core—which Lotman does not address.[37]

Instead, his moral judgment is hidden within his semiotic analysis. Recall the story of the corrupt brigade commander, Ponomarenko, forcing the "good" battalion commander Pastushenko into a disciplinary bind. Lotman tells the story as a semiotic parable, not a tale of defunct ethics. We discover which forces are acting upon these officers, what motivates their actions and upon what their actions have effect. The "drunken fool" Ponomarenko wants decorations, this leads him to give poor orders to the battalion commander Pastushenko, which results in the loss of men and a weakening of the battery. This string of events reveals the organizing structure of one small section of the army. It shows how information is both generated and communicated, how transformed when passing through varied parties with varied motivations; it reveals the effects of that communication. Pastushenko's psychology appears here as one element affecting a system of signification—as does Ponomarenko's vanity, and his propensity for alcohol. Subjected to the pressure of war, language reveals a spiritual paradigm for Tolstoy; the same literary experiment reveals a linguistic paradigm for Lotman. Even corruption has a crucial semiotic dimension.

There is a pattern discernable in Lotman's description—a pattern in which details reverse expectations. In Viktor Shklovsky's 1928 monograph *Material and Style in the Novel War and Peace*, certainly familiar to Lotman, Shklovsky points out that Tolstoy reverses certain details in his own war writing.[38] One example comes from the "Sevastopol" stories, where wounded men tend to think they've been killed, while men on the brink of death tend to believe they've only been lightly wounded. Shklovsky describes a Tolstoyan device: close attention to historical detail, followed by a reversal of the "direction" of that detail. According to Shklovsky, in Tolstoy's "historical" writing, the subjective value of the experience is inverted while the

---

37 Tolstoy, Leo. "Sevastopol in December." *Tolstoy's Short Fiction: Revised Translations, Backgrounds and Sources, Criticism.* Trans. Michael R. Katz. New York: Norton, 1991. 13-14

38 Shklovskii, Viktor. *Mater'ial i stil' v romane L'va Tolstogo "Voina i mir."* Hague: Mouton, 1970. 104.

objective details are taken straight from historical materials. Shklovsky sees in this technique a distinct mark of Tolstoy's war writing. We find the same Tolstoyan feature in Lotman: he too reverses the "direction" of certain details. His portraits of wintertime on the front are harrowing, but he slips a positive effect into the same sentence, and the winter suddenly becomes "our own," a figure of familiarity and benevolence. A similar, if opposite, moment of reversal takes place in the description of summertime: it's "warm . . . you can change your clothes"—when suddenly this idyll is interrupted by the invasion of parasites: you can ". . . beat your lice."

In Tolstoy, the lice infestation facilitates a spiritual awakening in the imprisoned Pierre Bezukhov. In Lotman, body lice don't serve any moral or spiritual purpose. His technique of "reversing" details serves the semiotic: each of these reversals troubles the easy link between signifier and its most obvious signified. For Lotman, war both reveals and generates semiotic systems and collisions.

* * *

Non-Memoirs—and Lotman's relation to it—consistently appears in the situation of breaking with old convention and participating in the cultivation of a new tradition. We see an instance of this dynamic phenomenon as Lotman forgoes a classic coming-of-age war narrative and instead finds his *Bildung* in a community of Pushkin scholars. We see another in the questions of form and genre his memoirs raise, as he plays with the tension between oral and written war stories, borrowing from Viktor Nekrasov and Aleksandr Tvardovsky. And though Lotman indisputably narrates in a Tolstoyan tradition, his debts to Tolstoy are complicated by his semiotic method. Indeed, much of his inheritance from Tolstoy comes in the guise of iconoclasm: a "reversal" of details, an interrogation of traditional historiographic logic, a focus on the non-heroic.

Rooted in literary tradition while simultaneously reinventing it, the poetics of Lotman's *Non-Memoirs* accord with his vision of the historical pace of scholarship. "A snake sheds its skin when it grows," he observes at the very end of *Non-Memoirs*. "This is a perfect sym-

bolic expression of scholarly progress." Lotman argued that the development of culture itself followed this path of growing and shed-
ding, constantly changing and yet always retaining self-consistency
in that evolution. "No matter how sad the individual moments of
this process are, it is not only inevitable, but necessary," he claims,
acknowledging the gravity of finding tradition and the necessary,
corollary tradition of breaking it. "All that remains is to hope that the
snake, having shed its skin, changed its color, and increased its size,
will still preserve the very unity of itself."

Caroline Lemak Brickman
Evgenii Bershtein

Analysis of the Poetic Text. Trans. D. Barton Johnson. Ann Arbor: Ardis, 1976.

Semiotics of Cinema. Trans. Mark E. Suino. Ann Arbor: University of Michigan Press, 1976.

The Structure of the Artistic Text. Trans. Gail Lenhoff and Ronald Vroon. Ann Arbor: University of Michigan Press, 1977.

The Semiotics of Russian Culture. With Boris Uspensky. Ed. Ann Shukman. Ann Arbor: University of Michigan, 1984.

Universe of the Mind: A Semiotic Theory of Culture. Trans. Ann Shukman, introduction by Umberto Eco. London & New York: I. B. Tauris & Co Ltd., 1990

Culture and Explosion. Trans. Wilma Clark. Ed. Marina Grishakova. Berlin: Mouton de Gruyter, 2009.